An Unyielding Woman

Ron Emond

Order this book online at www.trafford.com
or email orders@trafford.com

Most Trafford titles are also available at major online book retailers.

Printed in the United States of America.

ISBN: 978-1-4269-1659-5 (sc)
ISBN: 978-1-4269-8386-3 (e)

Trafford rev. 10/05/2012

 www.trafford.com

North America & international
toll-free: 1 888 232 4444 (USA & Canada)
phone: 250 383 6864 ♦ fax: 812 355 4082

DEDICATION

To my wonderful and loving wife Gina, who had to tolerate
my emotional character over the years that it took me to write this
story. Her confidence in me, gave me the strength to go on.

Foreword

This true story is based on interviews with the unyielding woman and the author's recall of his part in her life as her son.

The main character in this story is Toni, whose birth name was Antoinette. She was one of seven children born into a lower middle class New England lifestyle on November 10th 1908. Her father was European of French and Spanish extraction, which had fled to Canada and later to America with his parents after the outbreak of WW1. He ruled his house like the typical European patriarch who believed that women were servile. Her mother also French, was born in the United States in a small New England community. There is little known of her, except that she was an attractive quiet lady who was subservient to Toni's father. She died of a stroke before her fiftieth birthday.

The character and knowledge that Toni developed early in life, with only an eighth grade education, far exceeded that of many young people who completed their schooling. She never allowed the lack of schooling to get in the way of her education.

The intrepidity and common sense with which she faced life allowed her to overcome more adverse situations than most humans would be willing to endure. This biography of Toni's triumphs in life, as a female teen, a widowed mother, a single attractive lady in the working world and a true minority of the times in New England, both in gender and ancestry, should be helpful to Those readers who feel that life owes them something.

There are three main characters in this biography, Toni, Whitey and Ray. Toni's parents, brothers and sisters, as well as a few of her friends will also be mentioned on occasion. Whitey, a rugged out door adventurer was Toni's first love. Ray, a handsome well- educated man torn between the priest-hood and domestic life, was her first husband.

Until age 11, Toni's life seemed typical of a child growing up on a small farm. It was not until her completion of the eighth grade, that her life began to make a drastic change.

Chapter 1

Toni's story begins in the spring of 1921 when a New England family is up at dawn preparing to partake in their individual chores typical to living on a small farm. The growth and limited industry in the small community called Greenville, where they reside, is not what one would say is very progressive.

Unless the head of a household is employed full time in the bleachery, or works for the state, or in the township, farming is the next best way to put food on the table. The hours are long, and those in the family who are still in school, perform their duties before and after school hours. Those who are not attending school, toil in the fields and the barn from dusk till dawn. A pretty young lady, baptized Antoinette and nick named Toni by her brother Roland, works very hard along side of her brother as they reap from the land and their animals all that is possible for survival and profit for the family.

There are eight members in the family, including mom and dad.

Toni is third from the oldest out of four girls and two boys. Roland is the oldest.

School is out, the sun is bright and there is freshness in the air that gives one the feeling of a new inner self after a long winter sleep. The trees are covered with fresh young buds, and the ground cover is no longer a carpet of white fluff, but one of many colors. Mother Nature has redecorated for the new season.

Toni's teacher is standing on the porch of the one room schoolhouse waving, as Toni is yelling back to her, "I will see you after the summer vacation, Mrs. Johnson." As this pretty girl, in a dress made from burlap, that had been sewn and dyed dark blue by her mom, strolled along the dirt path to her home, happiness was projected to those who walked with her. Toni knew that she had many chores to do and very little time to play when she got home, but she loved life and very seldom felt a reason to complain. Little did she know that her father, Ovid (short for Ovidia), was going to pull her out of school and make her work on the farm with Roland, not allowing her to return to school at summers end. This would also be a surprise to Toni's mother.

That summer was typical for the family. They worked hard all week including Saturdays and were free to enjoy Sundays after church, playing games around the farm or going to the lake.

The summer months seemed to end quickly and Toni along with her sisters began thinking about school. It was when Ovid overheard Toni and her mother discussing what she would wear the first day of high school that he mercilessly bellowed out, "I have made a decision to pull Toni from school and have her help Roland with the chores around the farm." Speechless, Toni and her mother looked at each other in astonishment. Before Toni could speak, her mother gave her a sign to remain quiet as she approached her husband and asked "Are you making a joke?", knowing right well that Ovid very seldom laughed, and rarely joked on any subject.

"I am not joking and I do not wish to discuss the matter", Ovid responded. The decision has been made and that is final." Emily and Toni attempted to reason with him, but in no uncertain terms, they were told "to shut up and drop the subject.

Toni ran to her room in tears with her mom behind her. She wept in her mother's arms until she fell asleep. There was nothing short of a violent break up between Emily and Ovid that could be done. Toni's siblings of course feel that this is unfair, but knowing the wrath of Ovid they choose not to speak out for he was the typical fearful patriarch of that era.

He would think nothing of making their lives and their mothers and Toni's even more miserable if they dared to show him disrespect, even if it were appropriate at the time, so life as it was in their home continued on.

It was generally understood that the oldest boy in the family would have to help out on the farm, even if he did have to drop out of school, but for Ovid to pull Toni was cold and calculating.

Chapter 2

It was through this plot that Ovid had attempted to fulfill his inane desire to get even with Emily, Toni's mother, on the questionable assumption that she had an affair with a doctor who had been coming to their home to treat Ovid when he was down with pneumonia. Ovid had invented in his own mind that Toni could have been conceived at no other time, but during the two weeks he had been down with pneumonia, while his doctor had been making house calls.

Toni received her nickname from Roland, because she was so competitive in work and play, and could milk cows, pitch hay, cut wood, climb trees and fish as well as any boy in the area. She was a tomboy. She soon settled into her new way of life, still unaware why her father had chosen to single her out from her other three sisters. Each day she would rise at dawn, while the others were dressing for school, and happily head for Roland's room.

"Hey Roland," she would yell at his door. Common sleepy head, let's go before Pa gets mad and doesn't let us have breakfast."

"I'm coming," Roland responds as he hops from his room pulling on his other shoe. Anyway, if Pa doesn't let us eat, I will grab some crackers on the way to the barn and we will eat them with some of that fresh molasses out of the barrel that we mix in the cow's mash. I like that better than oatmeal any day!"

Toni, dressed in her bib overalls, plaid shirt, and rubber boots, confidently tags along behind her big brother toward the kitchen. As they approach, they can hear Ovid say to their mom "When is the last time you made fresh bread? When I set down to the dinner table this evening, I will expect fresh baked bread."

Roland turned to Toni, grabs her overall strap and pulls her along saying "To the barn," as he grabs a handful of crackers from the pantry shelf on their way out. Sometimes, they had to go out and milk the cows before breakfast, especially if Ovid demanded fresh milk.

"Boy! Am I glad Pa didn't want fresh milk this morning" says Toni, while she and her brother leaned against the sunny side of the barn eating crackers with fresh molasses from the barrel.

One day while they were cleaning the barn, Toni dispiritedly said to Roland. "I don't believe that Pa loves me, but I don't know why! What could I have done?"

Roland, knowing why, could only say, "Oh he loves you! He just doesn't know how to show it. Someday he will come around." Toni accepted her big brother's answer with a smile, and went on with her chores.

Chapter 3

In the spring it was plowing, planting, watering, feeding and whatever else was necessary at the time. In the summer the chores included the continuous gardening, as well as maintaining the barn, the corrals and various structures on the property, and feeding the animals. When fall came, it always seemed to be the toughest time of year. This was when the farmers had to finish getting in crops, and preparation for winter was the priority. Toni worked along side of her brother, quite often to the edge of exhaustion. Seeking admiration from Ovid, who sometimes worked close by, Toni would work harder then should be expected, hoping for a show of recognition by the man she loved as her father. At times, when Ovid would be within the sound of her voice Toni would ask, "How am I doing Pa?"

"Just keep your mind on your work," he would respond.

Holding back her tears, she continued working quietly, as she was well aware that her father could be extremely cruel, after watching him pull Roland from the back of their plow horse and beat him with a horse whip. Toni, also having felt the same whip when she spilled a pale of milk, was careful not to antagonize Pa. Soon autumn had arrived and the summer colors of red, green and purple had changed to yellow and gold. The nights were getting cool, and soon it would be time to heat the house by the wood stove and the fireplace.

It was an evening of the first week in September; the family was having supper and the kids were happily chatting back and forth. Ovid, looking at Toni and Roland, bellowed out, "You two had better start hauling some wood for the winter, if you want to have a warm house." In the next breath, before any response could be made, as he stood to leave the table, he said "And don't ask to use the horse, find some other way to haul out the logs." He then walked off.

Toni, looking at Roland, said, "We had better start tomorrow, right after we milk the cows."

Emily, feeling sorry for them, but unable to confront Ovid, said, "Your sisters and I will clean up the table and do the dishes."

You two get to bed early, so that you will be rested for a hard day tomorrow." Toni and her brother went off to bed, knowing that they had better get wood cut and stacked for the winter, which would be easier then facing their father's wrath.

The next morning, Toni woke Roland up, in her customary pleasant way, "Pa is still in bed! So what will it be, some French toast with mom's fresh bread in a warm kitchen, or crackers and molasses in the cold barn? She asked.

"You know the answer to that silly question!" Roland responded as they rushed to the kitchen and ate before Ovid came down.

Finishing quickly, they headed out into the brisk morning air. After milking the cows, they gathered their tools and headed for the low land at the back of the farm, where there were twenty foot logs, some a foot in diameter, that had been cut and left to dry a year prior. As they strolled along on the beautiful crisp morning, while watching the squirrels running up and down trees, gathering acorns for the winter, they schemed on a way to haul out those heavy logs. Roland had thought ahead and brought along two lengths of rope, he was sure would come in handy, since Pa said they could not use the plow horse, for pulling.

Roland made them each a shoulder harness to which one end would be tied to a log that they could pull to the area where they would be cutting them into shorter lengths. Sometimes, the two of them would haul together on the larger logs. That entire day, except for a short lunch break, they dragged logs over one hundred yards where they could eventually be cut into firewood. Roland would always see to it that Toni's rope was tied to the smaller logs, and he would pull on the ten and twelve inch diameter. When they were harnessed up, they would race to the upper pasture laughing as they sang "Oh! The old gray mare ain't what she used to be, Ain't what she used to be. Ain't what she used to be. OH! The old gray mare ain't what she used to be. so early in the morrr-ninn." The two of them hauled logs until dusk.

After dinner that evening, Toni bathed and was putting ointment on her shoulders, where the rope had caused blistering, when her Mom walked in. Seeing the abrasions, Emily asked, "Why didn't you tell me this at dinner?"

"Because I knew that I could handle it, and I didn't want you to say anything to Pa."

After comforting Toni, Emily went to Ovid, "I don't like what you are doing to our daughter, and it has to stop." she said aggressively, while he sat in his over stuffed chair reading a Zane Gray book.

"She is not our daughter she is yours, and as long as she lives under this roof she will do as I say and that is final!" Ovid bellowed back. Fortunately, Toni did not hear his reply. Emily called to Toni so that Ovid could see her blistered shoulders, and never taking his eyes from the book, he simply said "She will be fine in a few days."

Tears filled Emily's eyes, as she looked in Toni's direction. "I can handle it mom, it is no big deal." Toni replied as she gave her mother a hug and went off to bed. Emily quietly went to the living room and began mending the children's cloths. The others were either in bed or doing school work, and were oblivious to the situation.

That next morning, Roland had to get Toni out of bed. She was literally worn out. Standing against her bedroom door, so as not to be heard by Ovid, he quietly said "Common sis it is time to get up. Let's get started before Pa comes down to breakfast. You know how grumpy he is in the morning."

Opening her door, Toni said, "I'm getting ready, but my shoulders are so sore, it hurts to raise my arms."

Helping his sister to raise the shoulder straps of her bib overhauls, Roland could see that she was hurting and he felt bad, but he also knew that if she stayed in her room, Pa would cause her to wish she never had. "Get ready." he said. We will stay out of Pa's sight as much as possible, and you can set on the logs to hold them steady on the saw horse, while I cut them." Once enough logs were hauled up, Toni and her brother would hand saw them into two-foot lengths, with a cross cut two person saw, but today, Roland would do the sawing alone.

After a day of light work, some ointment on her shoulders and a good sleep, Toni was up and ready to go again. She and her brother cut wood that week, until they had eight to ten cords stacked by the house, which would get them through winter. It was a chore they were happy to have out of the way for one more year.

Quite often, after a long hard day, Toni would go straight to a bath without dinner and on to bed, where she read until she fell asleep. It was after one of those exhausting days, that she could hear her father and mother arguing, as she tried to read. Her mother had been trying to reason with Ovid about allowing Toni to go back to school.

With the scant assertiveness that Toni's mom was able to muster up, she attempted to intimidate Ovid. "Why are you singling out Antoinette? What has she ever done to you? She has always done as you have asked and seldom seeks recognition."

Without the slightest expression of empathy, in a spiteful tone, "She is my bastard daughter and you are lucky that I allow her to live under my roof. You conceived her when I was in bed with pneumonia. She is someone else's kid!" he bellowed.

Toni now new why her father treated her badly and though she was extremely hurt, she made up her mind not to let her mother or Ovid know what she overheard.

Emily ran to the bedroom in tears and sobbing. Hearing this, Toni wanted to go to her mother, but realized if she did, the situation could only worsen. Toni quietly speculated about what was said, and sobbed deeply, until she fell asleep.

Day after day, Toni's heart ached from the hurt her father had caused to her and her mother, but she did not allow Ovid the satisfaction of realizing this.

Roland hated his father for what he was doing to Toni, but there was nothing he could do about it.

He did not want to break his favorite sister's spirit, so he kept quiet, and told his other sisters to also keep quiet if they new what was good for them. They had heard Ovid accuse their mother of adultery when she became pregnant with Toni. Not wanting to believe what she heard the night before, Toni waited until she and Roland were working in the barn and no one else was around. "Did you know that Pa thinks I am the daughter of another man?" she asked.

Roland with an astonished look responded "Where did you hear that! Which one of our sisters told you that?"

"No one told me! I overheard Pa accusing mom!"

"How long have you known? Roland asked." Wanting to let his sister down easy, he said, "We heard Pa accuse mom of the same lie the day she told him that she was pregnant with you. We had all agreed to never say anything more about it. I still want to know how you found out."

Sadly, Toni said, as she began to cry, "I heard them arguing about it last night."

Holding her tightly, Roland said "It is all a lie that Pa has dreamed up, and you need to put it behind you, because no one believes him anyway. Remember, I will always be here for you."

Toni seemed comfortable with that.

Chapter 4

For the past two years Toni's father had been working for the New England Power Co., as a turbine operator.

These turbines produced the electricity on which the trolley cars were propelled. The income he earned, supplemented that which could not be covered by the farm income until 1925 when the trolley car system came to a halt, and several employees, including Ovid were let go. For a month or so, life in Toni's family became even more stressed, until Ovid found employment at the Greenville bleachery. Toni and her brother still continued to do the brunt of the farm work.

It wasn't long after Ovid received a few pay checks from his new job, when he concluded that the farm was not producing enough income to subsidize the difference needed, between his check and what it cost to take care of his family, so he told Toni and Roland that they had to go find employment, and start contributing to the household expenses. Needless to say, the two of them were very excited with the idea that they could actually start earning real money since they were only given twenty five cents a week for the farm work.

Toni got a job wrapping the bleached cloth for shipping, at the Bleachery where Ovid was working. They rode to and from work together, and few words were spoken, only out of necessity.

Roland took a job in a cloth printing shop in Providence, as a trainee. They were each allowed to keep one dollar a week, from their pay, for their personal needs. The remainder of their earnings went to the household. The other six children were allowed to continue with their education, and helped around the farm occasionally, but none of them were ever called on to work like Toni and Roland.

Chapter 5

By the time she turned sixteen, Toni developed a strong character. She acted as if the favoritism shown to her sisters and baby brother, Raymond, was nonexistent. Toni knew that her mother loved her very much, and this, with the support of Roland, was the corner stone of much of her strength.

On her sixteenth birthday, Emily gave Toni a coming out party, which her father did not attend. Her sisters and brothers were there, with some of Toni's old friend's she had made, prior to dropping out of school. Everyone got along well, as they played games, teased each other and talked of their futures. "What do you want to do when you get to adulthood?" one of them asked Toni.

"I hope to marry a nice man and grow old together, after raising our children."

"Do you want to live on a farm?" another friend asked.

"OH No!" Toni said, as she chuckled and looked over at her mom, who was smiling back at her. I have done enough farm work. I want to live in a big house in the country, with a green lawn and huge shade trees, so my husband and I can cuddle under them on a warm summer day, and watch the children play."

Toni's mom interrupted. "Come help me in the kitchen. I am sure that everyone must be getting hungry."

While Toni and her mom were preparing the plates of finger

snacks, and chatting, Emily said "Don't you think that it is about time you learned to dance?"

"Mom!" With laughter in her voice, "I do know how to dance," Toni responded. Roland and I have been practicing in my room ever since we no longer had to work on the farm, all day. He has been going over to Waterman's Lake Lodge to the Saturday night square dances, and says he has a great time. He has even promised to take me with him, as soon as I am old enough."

"Well! I think that you are old enough now," said Toni's mom. "Next Saturday you can go with your brother. I have already spoken with him about it, and he said it would be OK. Anyway, this way I know that he will stay out of trouble, as long as you are there."

Toni couldn't believe her ears. "What about Pa? Won't he try to stop me?" she asked.

"Not to worry," her mother responded. "I told him that I was letting you go, and he only groaned, as he read his book."

Toni worked hard at the Bleachery and at home, giving Ovid no opportunity to stop her from going out on Saturday evenings. She loved dancing, and when Friday evening came around, Roland could expect to hear her say, "Will you take me with you to Waterman's tomorrow night, please, please?" Roland always gave in.

How could he say no to his tomboy sister who was becoming quite the young lady, and he had grown very fond of, as far as sisters go? Anyway, now that they had been going to Waterman's for over a month, Toni had become friends of some pretty cute seventeen and eighteen year old girls, and Roland enjoyed flirting with them. The girls didn't mind a bit, since Roland was six feet tall, with dark brown wavy hair, dark brown eyes, a strong build and a very good dancer.

Chapter 6

By the time Toni turned eighteen, she had become one of the most popular young ladies at Waterman's dance hall. Many young men tried to court her, but there was only one young man she had an interest in.

He was Fred White, or "Whitey" as he was called by many; a twenty three year old adventuresome young man who was easily liked by all who met him because of his pleasant personality and good looks. He was tall, broad shouldered, had a square jaw with blue eyes and a nice smile. Though Whitey was not known to brag, he would not hesitate to talk of his travels when asked to do so by those who were aware of his spirit for adventure. Saturday night at Waterman's, after having been away for at least thirty days, when he wasn't dancing, he could be found at a table telling the young and the old about his latest adventure somewhere across the sea. He especially enjoyed telling his stories if Tony was listening. At age twenty three, he had seen more of the world than most men twice his age and was proud of it.

It was the year 1919, when at sixteen Whitey lied about his age and joined the US Army Transport Service. By age twenty, his rank was Quartermaster, and by then, he had traveled on bodies of water that most Americans had never heard of. His quest was to be a high ranking ships officer, one day. When ever his ship returned to port at Providence, Whitey could sign himself off of the ship for a two or three week lay over, after a month or two at sea.

It was during his time off that he would be at Waterman's lake either paddling his canoe, or swimming the length of the lake. He was an excellent swimmer, and it showed in his physic which the young ladies on the beach quite often took note of as they giggled among each other. By 6:00 P.M. Saturday evening, he could be found primping to meet the lady he was seriously falling for. He made it a point to arrive at the dance hall early so he could greet Toni at the door. Inside he would escort her to the coatroom and assist her out of her coat. Hand in hand, they strolled toward the dance floor, where with a handsome smile,

"May I have this dance madam?" he would ask.

"Yes you may." she responded, and from then till midnight, the two of them danced and talked with an occasional break for a soda and to freshen up, only occasionally acknowledging Roland and friends. The two of them seemed inseparable for which Roland was pleased since he liked Whitey.

On Sunday Whitey would take Toni for a ride in his canoe, and paddle to a small island on the lake, where they would lay in the sun and affectionately talk of the future. Occasionally, Toni would allow Whitey to give her a kiss on her cheek. "When I make the rank of Second Mate and I am assigned to a major cruise line,

I will buy you whatever your heart desires." He would say, kissing her cheek lightly.

"Oh yeah, and when will that be? I don't want to wait until I am too old to have the things my heart desires." Toni responded jokingly, as she chuckled, jumped up from the blanket, and began walking in the direction of the lake.

Realizing that she was only teasing him, Whitey ran to her and picked her up as he said "It will be sooner than you think, so you had better be prepared to say yes, the day I come home from a voyage and ask you to marry me."

Toni knew that Whitey was serious, and she felt a strong affection for him, but was not thinking of marriage at her age. With a somber expression, she said "It is getting close to dinner time, we'd better get going."

Whitey recognizing the sudden change from joking to serious, "Have I said something wrong?" he questioned.

"No! I just think we need to get going." she said, smiling slightly. The paddle back to shore from the island was quiet, other than an occasional comment. "I am not looking forward to tomorrow. I wish that I didn't have to go to that hot Bleachery!"

On their way to Toni's house, they agreed to see each other as much as possible that following week, because Whitey was shipping out on Saturday. For the next two years, whenever Whitey was home, they spent as much time together as possible. While at sea, Whitey worked and studied hard. He not only had attained the rank of Chief Petty Officer, but was also well on his way to being promoted to Second Mate. He was half way to his goal, and earning a relatively good income for the times, and his age.

At sea, Whitey's letters to Toni were full of loving expression, as were hers to him. It was their timing that did not mesh. Toni felt that someday she would be Whitey's partner in marriage, but not for, at least two or three more years. He of course, thought differently.

Whitey's last assignment to a ship was the longest of his past two years. He had been at sea for over three months, and missed Toni very much. His thoughts of her took up all his spare time, so when he arrived home from his long tour, Whitey took a bus to the end of the route within a few blocks of the Bleachery, and ran the remainder of the distance, to see Toni. As he entered the office of the building, he tried to ignore the receptionist, but... "Sir, Sir, Where do you think you are going?" she asked.

Turning suddenly and looking into her eyes with a big smile, this man in his white uniform, with his officer's cap under his arm, said "I am going to give the lady I love a hug and a kiss."

The receptionist, seemingly embarrassed, said "oh" and looked away. When she looked back, Whitey was gone, and on his way to the department where Toni was working. The receptionist rolled her eyes and continued as if nothing had happened.

When Toni saw Whitey coming toward her, she thought of how handsome he looked in his summer white uniform as she trembled with excitement. A few of the other girls in the department whistled their appreciation of this handsome man in uniform, which Whitey responded to, with a salute. Toni, always the lady, grabbed his hand and led him to the coffee lounge, where they could embrace each other in private. "God I have really missed you." Whitey said. I have so much that I want to tell you."

"I have also missed you very much," said Toni, but we can't talk now. My boss will be coming by any minute. I get off in a few hours, and we can go somewhere quiet and talk."

Giving Toni a hug and a kiss on the cheek, Whitey departed and made it a point to tip his hat to the receptionist on the way out. "I should be so lucky." She quietly commented to herself.

That evening, the loving couple went to their favorite restaurant, where they sat at a quiet corner table, and held hands. After finishing a fine dinner, Whitey again placed his hand over Toni's and looking into her eyes, he said "Sweetheart I will be twenty six in a few months, and you will be… well, you know, we aren't getting any younger! What I am trying to say is,…" taking a small black box from his pocket and placing it in front of her, "Will you marry me?"

Opening the box and finding a sparkling diamond set in a gold band Toni's eyes filled with tears. "It is beautiful." She said as she grasped Whitey's hand tightly.

Hesitantly, as if thinking how she did not want to hurt the man she loved, Toni said "You know that I love you very much and in the future, I believe that we will one day be married, but I do not feel I am ready to take on that responsibility just yet. I need more time. Maybe in a year, but not just yet."

Obviously hurt, Whitey responds "Why?" "You say that you love me. Then why wait?"

"I don't know why, I just don't feel that I am ready yet. I am not interested in anyone else, but I need more time."

Heartbroken and realizing that he could not change Toni's mind, Whitey suggested that he take her home. He escorted Toni to her door, kissed her goodbye and departed with tears in his eyes.

He knew it would be best if he stayed away. The following day, he signed on the next ship over seas, and was not to be heard from again, for a long time.

Chapter 7

The year 1929 became a traumatic period in the lives of most of America. The period of the Great Depression, and the end of post war prosperity would soon come to an end. World War I, which had involved England, France and the United States against Germany, came to an end at the 1919 Paris Peace Conference. For the next ten years, the economy of the world was strong, creating a facade of wealth. Many Americans became rich, and many only acted the part, until October 29th 1929, when the stock market suddenly began to decline and the investors began pulling out their monies. The Federal Reserve, a privately owned banking system which controlled all of the tax payers monies, had pulled the plug on the investment market causing a panic that negatively affected the American economy for over ten years. Within days, banks began failing, and soon the country fell into what is now known as the "Great Depression". Many of the investors, who were only millionaires on paper, committed suicide. By 1932, 12 million Americans were unemployed.

Like so many, Toni's home was also feeling the effect of the depression. Ovid was working only ten hours a week, so there was less money to pay bills and feed his large family. Many times, the meals consisted of potato soup, and a piece of bread. Sometimes they would have one meal a day, but they considered themselves lucky, since they still had their small farm and could grow a few vegetables, and have an occasional egg and a glass of milk, from the one cow and the few chickens that were left. The other animals had to be sold or traded for things the family needed.

Toni's aunt Adie, short for Adeline, on her mother's side, an outgoing, fun loving middle aged realist, who seemed to be handling the stock market crash better than most had become a widow just prior to the crash and was living alone. Adie was well aware that her sister was having it tough, both financially and domestically, so she suggested that Toni move in with her to help relieve some tension on the domestic situation that still existed between Toni and Ovid. "Why don't you let Toni come and live with me? After all, I live alone in that big house, and I would enjoy the company! The place is getting to be quite much for me to keep up, and Toni would be a big help."

Hearing this, Toni looking at her mother, excitedly expressed her desire to go with her aunt. "Mother, I would really like to move in with Aunt Adie. I can be of help and a companion to her and it would be one less mouth to feed around here."

"I don't know!" exclaimed Emily.

"Why not?" Ovid responded. She would be closer to her job." Adie, realizing Ovid's ulterior motive, looked at her sister

and said "Why not?"

Toni's mom nodded her head with a smile, and said, "Ok" as

she hugged Toni briefly. Toni was delighted, but since her and her sister Agnes had grown close, she asked if Agnes could also move to Adie's with her.

Emily shrugged her shoulders and smiled as she looked at

Adie in agreement. "The more the merrier." Adie said, and with this, Toni and Agnes gave their mom and aunt a hug, after expressing a cordial thanks to their father.

That week, the ladies moved to their new home, where

they had their own rooms. To them, Aunt Adie's house was mansion. The two story yellow and white Victorian, with its green lawns and rose bushes, gave the appearance that proud and successful people lived there. The floor above the basement consisted of a large kitchen, formal dinning room, living room, cozy sitting room, den and a washroom. Upstairs there were four bedrooms and a washroom.

The house had been built by Adie's husband, an architect, who had died of a heart attack at the age of forty one.

Fortunately, he had left a large amount of cash in the house safe, so Adie was not affected by the fall of the stock market, and she could live better than most during the hard times. She did not flaunt her comfort and was charitably smart. The girls settled in quickly, and even though the little town of Greenville demonstrated the effect of the depression, they and their aunt made each day a cheerful one.

The hours at the bleachery were cut to a minimum, so Toni and Agnes had quite a bit of free time, and used it wisely. When they finished with their duties at aunt Adie's, they quite often did volunteer work for the church. Adie believed strongly, that there is a higher power, and she supported the girl's involvement in the church, especially if it was charitable. Adie, a stylish lady in her own right, never shunned someone in need, and avoided the snobbery of the fake upper class.

Needless to say, with their aunt as their mentor, Toni and Agnes matured into quality ladies who drew many second glances from the young men. They continued to spend most of their Saturday evenings at Waterman's, and kept in mind, Adie's advice. "A lady not only looks the part, but also acts it, no matter the circumstances."

They knew how to be refined, and when to let their hair down for some fun, but still remain chic. They had no problem meeting men, and Agnes soon met a man she felt comfortable with.

Toni was comparing all men to Whitey, and was obviously still pining for him, though she had not heard from him since the night before he left. She was aware that he was far out to sea, but had no idea where, nor when he might return. She could only hope that if and when he came back to Greenville, he would call on her. Seeing this in Toni, Adie encouraged her to continue her favorite Saturday night entertainment at Waterman's.

Chapter 8

Agnes's boyfriend was Bill Donahue, a descent looking young man from a nice middle class family. He had a car and it got them around, even though it wasn't much to look at. On Saturday, at seven thirty sharp, Bill would drive to Adie's for the girl's. They could hear him coming two blocks away, because the car needed a muffler. "Here comes Bill." Agnes would yell to Toni.

"Oh how embarrassing! When is he going to get that muffler repaired?" Toni responded.

Adie, chuckling loudly, "I know that I had a lot to do with teaching you refinement, but I hope it is not causing you to become a snob. I remember a young lady who thought wrestling with her big brother and hanging upside down in a tree with her bloomers showing was perfectly All right. Now you are embarrassed by a loud muffler? Remember, even though you are a lady, that does not guarantee you a free ride. Why don't you chip in for a new muffler?"

I happen to like Bill's car, so let's go!" Agnes said, as she grabbed Toni's hand, and pulled her out the door.

The dance ended at eleven, and Bill always suggested ice-cream, before going home. It was on one of those evenings, that Toni's life was suddenly dangling in a life or death situation.

The time was approximately twelve P.M.

They were at the ice-cream parlor, when they heard a loud "Hey, how are you guys doing?" It was Joe Broadbent, a friend of Bill's. Joe a boisterous, sometimes obnoxious individual liked Toni and did his damnedest to impress her. Toni was always cordial, but never led him on. She respected him as a friend, and did not hesitate to let him know that she still cared for Whitey. Joe had hoped this would change with time, and did not try to force his affection on her.

After a few laughs and a dish of ice-cream, the four of them agreed that they should be getting home. "Hey Joe, I bet you wouldn't mind taking Toni home, would you? Bill asked with a smirk on his face, and tapping Joe on the shoulder. Agnes and I want to be alone."

Like a child getting a piece of candy, Joe of course jumped at this opportunity. "No I don't mind a bit, but it is up to Toni."

Realizing that her sister would also like some time alone with Bill, Toni said "I will go on the condition that you take me straight home, with no detours."

Bill and Agnes, hoping to lose Joe and be alone for a while, drove away quickly. Joe had a faster car, and soon caught up with Bill. The roads were very narrow and without lighting, except for the vehicle's headlights which were like trying to light a ballroom with two candles. The road surface was gravel and not suitable to fast driving, but racing over them was just another pastime for Bill and Joe.

When Bill saw that he was being pursued by Joe, he began slowing to motion Joe to back off. Thinking that he could impress Toni, Joe stayed extremely close to the back of Bill's vehicle and pressed on his horn. This activity even seemed like fun to Toni for while, but not to Bill, so he increased his speed, as did Joe.

At speeds up to seventy miles per hour, what was supposed to be a leisure drive home had now become a race to feed the male ego? Toni soon became frightened, "Slow down! Slow down before we get into an accident." she said. But Joe did not slow the vehicle.

"Hold on! I will pass him on the straight section up ahead and then slow down before we get to your house." Joe responded. Toni's face was strained with fear, as she reached into her purse and clutched the rosary that she always carried. Her intuition was telling her that something serious was about to happen.

The race had continued for over four miles, when they came to a long straight stretch in the road where Joe felt he could pass Bill up. Their speed had decreased to about fifty five miles per hour because of a curve just before the straight section, but now seventy or seventy five was not out of the question, so Joe began to accelerate as did Bill. Joe's car seemed to increase its speed more quickly and soon his right front wheel was passing Bill's left rear. They covered about a quarter of a mile as Joe continued to slowly move up on his opponent, when suddenly, head lights appeared to be coming directly at Joe from about one hundred yards away. The vehicle had pulled out from a side road. "Oh shit!" said Joe, as he realized that he did not have time to complete his attempt to pass Bill.

Focusing on the vehicle coming at him, Joe decelerated and hit his brakes, causing his vehicle to pull slightly to the right. Neither vehicle had mud guards (fenders) since they were removed by the owners because it lightened the vehicles for speed, and it looked racy. As Joe's vehicle moved to the right, his right front tire became tangled inside of Bills left rear and both vehicles began to loose control. The action of the tires locking caused Bill to come left into a spin and out into a field right side up. Joe's car jerked to the right, and as he tried to correct, it spun back to the left and rolled over. It rolled once and began to roll again, when Toni's door flew open and she was thrown out. The car rolled twice more and came to a rest upside down, with Joe inside.

Bill and Agnes, shaken, but otherwise All right, ran back to Joe's car, where they found him crawling out the rear window. "Joe! Are you ok?" asked Bill.

"I think so." Joe responded, as he brushed himself off. He was bleeding from the mouth and obviously had several abrasions and bruises, but miraculously had suffered no broken bones.

Agnes looked under the upside down car for Toni and hysterically began to scream. "Where is my sister, my sister, where is she?" They could not see Toni in the darkness and began looking for her frantically. "Toni, Toni. Where are you?" they called out, but to no avail. Each of them ran in separate directions calling and searching in the darkness.

The car that had been coming the other way had of course stopped, and after ascertaining the situation, sped on to get help.

It seemed like hours, but in about twenty minutes, two police cars and an ambulance arrived. The officers directed their headlights and spot lights toward the right shoulder of the road, where after a short time, they spotted what appeared to be a depression in the high weeds about thirty feet beyond Joe's car and ten feet off of the gravel shoulder. "It looks as if there is something over there." said one of the officers, as he held his light on the depression, and they all ran to the area.

Joe got there first, and found Toni lying twisted and still. She was bleeding profusely from the left side of her head, near the temple. Joe took off his jacket and placed it over Toni to keep her warm, as he tried to communicate with her. "Toni can you hear me?" he said over and over, as the ambulance attendant felt for a pulse. "OH GOD Oh GOD what have I done?"

The ambulance attendant checked Toni's vital signs. "She is unconscious, and going into shock, we need to move her now." He emphasized. Toni was carefully moved to a stretcher and taken to the hospital.

It was later determined that when Toni was thrown from the vehicle, she had hit the pavement head first and then slid on her right side, more than twenty feet to where she was found.

The doctors at the hospital diagnosed a severe skull fracture with pressure on the brain, causing Toni to be in a coma. She also had very severe lacerations and abrasions that would most likely leave scars, but this was a minor concern. Toni's mother was called, and she arrived with Ovid and Aunt Adie. That night, Emily sat by her daughter's bed and wept, while Adie, Agnes, Joe and Bill slept in the waiting room.

Ovid stopped by the door, briefly looked in on Toni, and with a cold expression, said to Emily, "I will stop by tomorrow and talk with the doctor." He walked off.

The following morning Emily asked Toni's doctor for a prognosis, but he could only tell her, "A will to live and time are the best medicine in Toni's case. She will need your prayers more than ever now." He said. The next four days were very somber, as the family and friends stayed close by and prayed.

On the morning of the fifth day, with tears in his eyes, Roland held her hand, and said "Toni it's me, your big brother, you can't give up over a bump on the head. Hell you had worse bumps falling out of trees, and anyway, Waterman's won't be the same without you." Momentarily, he felt Toni squeeze his hand. "Did you see that?" he asked his mother and Adie, standing at the foot of her bed. "She squeezed my hand!" he said with tears running down his cheeks.

"I knew it I knew she would pull through." Adie responded. Emily walked to Toni's side and prayed silently, as she wiped her daughter's brow. Soon after, Toni opened her eyes and gazed at the light over her bed.

Seeing his sisters eyes open, Roland, excitedly called out "Nurse, call the doctor, my sister is awake!"

Toni still seemed to be in a daze when the doctor arrived. He checked her eyes and reflexes, as mom anxiously awaited. After the examination, the doctor informed Emily that he had some concern about the possibility of permanent brain damage, and until the swelling on her brain receded, he could not make an accurate diagnosis.

By the middle of the following week, Toni showed rapid progress. The swelling had diminished and all indications were, that she would fully recover, except for the possibility of some permanent scaring. The doctor was pleased. After almost three weeks in the hospital, Toni was told that she could go home, but when her mom and Roland came to get her she did not want to leave.

Her face was badly scared, and she had an obvious loss of hair over her right temple. "Let me stay here longer, at least until my hair grows back and my scars are not so distinct." Toni pleaded, as she lowered her head and began to sob.

Roland went for the doctor, and requested that he try to build up Toni's self confidence. "I will see what I can do." the doctor responded, as they walked back to her room. "Toni, Toni, Toni!" said the doctor, as he put his arm over her shoulders. Roland tells me that you do not want to leave. Why would you want to stay in this dull hospital, when there is so much for you to do on the outside?"

"But look at me doctor, I am ugly. If only I could stay here a little longer, at least until my hair grows back, then I wouldn't feel so bad." she responded.

Placing his hand under her chin, and looking into her eyes her doctor said, "What you are worried about is all superficial and will improve in time. Your hair will grow back fully, the scarring will fade, and you will remain beautiful. Now go with your mom and your brother, and I will see you next week." With this, Toni gave the doctor a smile and agreed to go home.

Home at her aunt Adie's, Toni would only allow her immediate family to see her. She believed in what her doctor had told her, and also believed that she had a responsibility to help her situation improve. Day after day, for six months, she applied the oils from the Aloe Vera plant to her scars. She brushed and massaged her scalp for at least an hour at a time. As her appearance Improved, so did her attitude about being seen in public, so she returned to work at the bleachery. Her perseverance in her resolution to completely eliminate the scaring ultimately resulted in very slight impressions that only Toni could see. She continued to have severe head aches, which the doctor told her would most likely plague her for years, but her strong character did not let that get her down.

Chapter 9

In the months to follow, Adie felt that introducing Toni to some of the finer things would add to the strong character she was known for, and still keep her soft and feminine. She was concerned that Toni might harden her outlook in life, as often happens when a person has to recover from a severe trauma, especially having been denied by their father as a child. Both Toni and Agnes were given guidance in etiquette and proper posture. Toni also joined an all women's orchestra, where she played the French horn.

Agnes chose to be with Bill as much as possible. In a few short months, the ladies developed a self confidence that got them even more attention from the men. Bill noted some what of a difference in Agnes's feelings toward him. She seemed to be enjoying the attention of other men, though she only dated Bill. With her trauma just about forgotten, Toni seemed to be on her way to establishing her self in the life of a single attractive lady. On occasion, Whitey would still come to her mind, and she would find herself wondering what he was up to. She still loved him.

Chapter 10

Whitey, by now, had become a full fledged Merchant Marine Officer, certified to stand at the controls, next to the captain, on great ships, like the Southern Cross, the Pan America and the world's largest oil driven ocean liner, the S.S. Leviathan. He had survived hurricanes and typhoons while sailing the North and South Pacific Oceans. His travels took him through the Panama Canal into the South Atlantic, around the Cape of Good Hope at the tip of South Africa, and into the Indian Ocean. From there, he traveled up to the Bay of Bengal to the coast of India. His adventures were non stop, and he loved every day of it. He was well respected by the crew both aboard ship and on shore.

He would often leave a ship that would be staying in a port for more than four or five days, and sign aboard one that would take him to places like Spain and Morocco. Whitey would try anything at least once. He experienced the opium dens in China, and fought over women in the bars of Casablanca and Madrid. He was considered tough and one hell of a man in the eyes of any Merchant Marine who new him. He was a gentleman first, and he had no tolerance for those in his company, who were not. When it came to the ladies, he seemed to always have the prettiest in each port. He made up his mind that if he couldn't have Tony as his wife he would remain a bachelor and enjoy each day of his adventuresome life to the fullest.

It was as if he was still attempting to fulfill the void in his heart, left there by Toni.

He remained over seas for two years signing on transport ships and tankers before returning to the states, where he spent a short time in New York, and then off to Europe again. Whitey never stopped thinking of Toni, but he would not humble himself to looking her up in fear of getting his feelings hurt. Toni, now twenty one years of age, has developed a strong, pleasant character. She still feels strongly for Whitey but has also accepted the fact that he may never return. Her time spent with men, is based on friendship only and getting into a serious relationship is the furthest thing from her mind.

Toni has learned to live with the fact that her father refused to accept her as his daughter. She accepts that there is a purpose for her existence, and has developed a very strong constitution for facing things that could cause her to think negatively.

Adie who fully intends to keep Toni from becoming an old maid is insisting that Toni meet a young man she has in mind, if for nothing else, but friendship. His name was Raymond, and he had been living at the La Salle Seminary, for the past three years, where he was studying to be a priest. He had begun questioning if the priest hood was to be his destiny, and made these feelings known to his brother. Dolor, Raymond's older brother, had met Adie when he and his wife were at a church gathering.

Dolor had become quite friendly with Adie's husband and they had been getting together to play cards, and doing men things, until her husband passed away. Dolor had met Toni at Adie's home, one Sunday afternoon, when he and his wife stopped by after church. It was during their conversation that Dolor spoke of his brother's quandary.

A few weeks later, Adie recalled that discussion, and in her mind set to find a male friend for Toni, she made it a point to see Dolor, at the church.

"Remember a short time ago when you told me about your brother's quandary to stay or leave the seminary?" she asked.

"Sure I do." said Dolor.

"Well I thought that it would be nice if Ray could meet Toni, and possibly make a change in his life, as well as hers."

"Good idea." responded Dolor.

Ray's mother was very self-centered, and her only concern was her status in the neighborhood. She often pressured her boys into doing things that drew attention to her. To have one of your boys become a priest, was looked at honorably, by friends and neighbors, so Ray became his mothers target for the priesthood. He never realized that he was being led to fulfill his mother's self-centered goal to reach the highest level of status in a Catholic neighborhood.

Knowing that Ray had entered the seminary more because of pressure from his mother, then by personal choice, Dolor hoped that Toni would be the one factor by which Ray would find himself. He and Adie began their little plot to arrange for a gathering by which the two young adults could meet.

The end of August and the sultry days soon will be turning to the crisp September sun shinny days. The leaves on the trees had begun to change and the forests that blanketed New England would soon turn to the beautiful red and gold colors which no quilt maker could ever duplicate. It is a time of year that is equal to spring for those romantic couples out for a stroll, or just sitting at a window, and gazing out at the striking colors that embellish the country side. The stage is set, and it is the perfect time for match making. The performers are all that is needed.

"Why don't you tell Ray that he is invited to a Sunday dinner, and get together, on the second Sunday in September," Adie suggested to Dolor.

"I'll do that, and if that doesn't fit his schedule at the seminary, I will let you know what day he can make it." He responded.

A few days later, Dolor drove to the seminary to meet with his brother and presented the invitation. Ray, never having met Adie, asked, "Why me, I don't even know this lady. She is your friend! He exclaimed...

"I just thought that you might like to get out of this inner sanctum, and meet some of my friends. After all, a short time ago, you told me that you are no longer sure that the priesthood is your calling. Come on, it will be a good change of pace." Dolor said as he smacked his brother on the back...

"Maybe you are right, when is this festivity going to take place?"

Ray asked... "If it fits your schedule, it is planned for the second Sunday in September."

"I will make it fit. Tell your friend I will be there, that is of course, if you can pick me up" Ray responded.

"Great" said Dolor, "Now let's go get some lunch at Luigi's, I'm buying."

With the stage set, and the performers invited, the plot was now in the hands of Adie and Dolor. Would their design to get Ray and Toni together, be a success? Only time would tell.

Chapter 11

The big day was soon here, and a dinner, consisting of roasted lamb, twice baked potatoes, carrots baked in brown sugar and butter, mint jelly, homemade biscuits, and Adie's famous sweet potato pie was the menu for that special Sunday afternoon. Toni, having no idea of her aunt's plans, asked, "Why all the frills, Aunt Adie? We have had guests for Sunday dinners before, but this is the first time that we have gotten so elaborate, since I moved in. Have you invited the Pope?" she said with a chuckle.

"No not the Pope, but someone who might take his place someday, unless he decides to seek a new vocation." Adie said, with a grin.

"Who did you invite, asked Toni, is he a priest?"...

"She may as well invite a priest, since you are going to end up a spinster anyway." said Agnes, who was helping to set up the dinning room. Ever since Whitey left, you haven't given another man a second glance.

"Well, I just haven't met one as good looking and exciting as Whitey." responded Toni.

"That is enough of the bickering you two. Our guests will be here soon, and I would like everything in order." said Adie.

Dolor, his wife Louise, and Ray soon arrived. Agnes's friend, Bill had arrived a few minutes before them, so that Agnes would have her own companion. All was going according to plan. Toni and Agnes had met Dolor and Louise when they visited previously, but introduction to the handsome dark stranger with them, was definitely in order.

As Adie took the coats of Dolor and Louise, Agnes wasted no time asking the stranger for his coat, flirtatiously saying, "Hello!" I am Agnes it is very nice to meet you."

Bill followed, shaking Ray's hand, and continued to where he could keep an eye on Agnes. Toni, less aggressive than her sister, when it came to men, waited to be introduced.

"OH honey, I am sorry!" Adie exclaimed as Toni stood there with a blank look on her face. I forgot that you and Ray had never met before. This is Dolor's brother, Raymond, who has been living at the LaSalle Seminary, where he is preparing to enter the priesthood. Ray this is my niece Antoinette, who is best known as Toni, by all who know her well. "The introduction couldn't have gone better if Adie and Dolor had planned it together. Ray and Toni had now become the center of attention.

After a few subtle niceties, in the living room, Adie invited everyone to the dinning room, where she just happened to see to it that Ray and Toni sat next to each other. Toni was understandably uneasy at first, but Ray's easy mannerism soon changed that, and during the course of dinner, it was obvious that they were hitting it off. Ray was dressed in light brown slacks, a forest green V-neck sweater, and dark brown shoes.

His casual attire and his mild mannerism caused Toni to comment, "You don't act or dress the part of a priest."

"Well I haven't made my final vows yet, so I am really not a priest, but what should a priest act like, anyway?" Ray asked.

"You know, stuffy, righteous and looks down his nose at you." said Toni.

"That is enough of that!" Adie said glaring over at Toni.

"That's Al right Adie, I know exactly what she means, and that is one of several reasons why I am considering leaving the Seminary." said Ray.

"Oh! If you do leave, when will that be?" asked Toni...

"That is hard to say. I have been at LaSalle for a little over three years, and that is the only life I really know as an adult. When I graduated catholic high school, I went to Brown University for two years, and then to the Seminary, so I want to be sure that whatever decision I make, is the right decision.".…

"So if you decide to become a civilian, will you date girls?" asked Agnes.

Kicking her under the table, "What do you care?" Bill asked. "I was just wondering." said Agnes, as everyone, except Bill,

chuckled.

"Yes Agnes, I believe that I would like to date a nice young

lady, if I decide to become a civilian, as you put it." Ray responded.

After dinner, everyone retired to the living room. Adie and Louise sat on the sofa, and Ray sat across from them in the high back chair, where he could use the matching foot stool. Ray and Toni made themselves comfortable on the love seat, while Agnes and Bill excused themselves and went out onto the veranda.

Toni was fascinated with Ray. After all, he was tall and good looking, but more than that, he was educated, and he made her feel like a real lady, with his gentlemanly way of talking to her.

The afternoon had gone as Adie had hoped, but it also went quickly, and before they realized, it was time for the guests to leave. Everyone expressed their good by's and soon the large house was very quiet. "Well, I guess I will clean up the kitchen and then go to bed." said Toni.

"I will help." said Agnes, following behind her sister.

"While you two are cleaning up, I think that I will set in

the living room and read a while." said Adie…

"Well?" said Agnes with a grin on her face as she worked with Toni.

"Well what?" Toni Responded.

"You know! What did you two talk about?"

"Not much, I just asked what it was like to be confined to the seminary with only men around, and why he chose the priesthood! He said, at times he feels confined and he has to get out, and there are other times that he enjoys the serenity of it all, but those times are happening less and less. He chose the priesthood, because he knew it would please his mother, and he also thought he felt a calling.

Now he is wondering if that feeling was brought on by his mother's intimidating way."

Ray recalls that his mother often reminded her boys, that she hoped one of her sons would be a priest. He now needs time to think, and clear his head, so he can decide if that is the life for him." Toni told Agnes.

"Do you think that he likes you?" Agnes asked.

"I don't know! It was easy to talk with him, and he did say that he may come again, with Dolor, in a few weeks. That's all I know." exclaimed Toni.

As Dolor drove home, he asked Ray "Did you enjoy yourself?"

"Yes! I did, it was nice to get out and be with nice people, other then my family, for a change. It has been almost a year since the last dinner engagement that I was invited to. That one was boring, compared to this one."

"What was so special about this get together?" Dolor asked?

"Everyone was congenial you know, easy to talk to. No one was pretentious, like that last group." Ray responded.

"Is that all?" asked Louise from the back seat, with a grin from ear to ear. Dolor, also smiling, winked at his wife, as he glanced at her in the rear view mirror.

"Well I have to admit, I found Toni very pleasant. She was easy to talk with and very attractive, but until I find my place in life, I have to keep things in there proper order, which you two have not made easy.

"Shall it be the priesthood or shall I become indigenous to the world of domestication?" "That is the question!" Asked Ray with a smile.

"We thought that this was just the thing you needed, to help you get through your dilemma. After all, how often have you sat next to a pretty lady in the past three years, and been able to talk in general, instead of listening to some pretentious fop, looking for an excuse to continue living a facade? You need to experience more life outside of the seminary, so that you can weigh the pros and cons realistically, to arrive at what is right for you." said Dolor.

In the weeks to follow, Ray visited Toni on three different occasions, which caused him to develop stronger feelings for her, but only made his dilemma more complicated. As a priest, Ray knew he would have food in his stomach, a warm place to lay his head, an allowance for clothing and spending money, not much, but as a priest, he would not need much cash anyway, and the opportunity to see many places in the United States and over seas, that few domesticated men would ever have the opportunity to visit. Was security the reason why he was hesitating to venture out and take on the challenges common to a domesticated man?

If his mother had not mentioned the priesthood so much, from the time he was a little boy, would he be in this predicament now?... These questions were buzzing around inside of Ray's head day and night. He loved his mother as any man should, and he wanted to please her. He realized that she would be very upset if he left the seminary, but he also had himself to live with. Ray had less than five weeks to decide his future, because at the end of that time period, he would begin to prepare for his final vows and the acceptance of the priesthood. Out of desperation, he chose to stay secluded, at the seminary and pray for guidance.

Toni having developed strong feelings toward Ray, and aware that she could be getting into an impossible situation, refused to allow herself to become over anxious about seeing him again,... other than in a friendly sort of way. When they last saw each other, she had a feeling that Ray might go into seclusion, and she told him, if nothing else, they could always be friends.

Thanksgiving was just a few weeks away, and Toni had pretty much accepted that Ray had made a decision to stay with the seminary, when in the mail came an envelope addressed to her.

Adie, having received the envelope, handed it to Toni with a smile, saying, "I have a feeling that this is good news."

Realizing whom it was from; Toni anxiously tore open the envelope and became engrossed in its contents. A gentile smile came over her pretty face, as she looked at her aunt Adie, "Ray has made the choice to leave the seminary. He has decided to seek a profession outside of the religious field, and will be coming to see me soon."

As Adie gave her niece a hug, she said "I knew it. I knew it! I felt all along, that you two were meant for each other, so I prayed that God would free up Ray's mind so he could think straight and choose you."

"We are just good friends, It's not like he has proposed to me," Toni responded.

"He will! You just wait," said Adie.

Chapter 12

The Thanksgiving and Christmas holidays were just around the corner, and the thought that her and Ray could be together for those fun days excited Toni beyond expectation. She was obviously falling hard for Ray. He had visited twice since his letter to her, and would have visited more, had he a vehicle. He was living with Ray and Louise, over an hour away by car.

A bus traveled to Greenville from the town where Dolor's home was located, but since Ray had not found a job yet, he could only afford to see Toni twice a week.

He was proud, and refused charity from his brother, who had offered to bank roll him until he was gainfully employed. He was paying Dolor for his room and board out of a small savings, and expected to be employed any day. Accounting was Ray's forte. He was brilliant with numbers, and could add three columns of figures, five in each column, in his head, and give the correct answer in a matter of seconds.

Yellow Cab, the largest commercial people mover of its type on the East Coast, had his application, and there was a good chance that he would be hired as the head accountant in their Providence office. Ray had already been interviewed twice, and the final interview was to take place after Thanksgiving.

Toni invited Ray to her aunt Adie's home for Thanksgiving, which he, of course, accepted. He knew that he could go to his parents home with Dolor and Louise, but he also realized that his mother would make life miserable, not only for him and Dolor, but also Toni, and he was not about to place her in such an ugly situation.

Rays mother was extremely displeased with the fact that the only opportunity to have a son in the priesthood had been destroyed. When Ray brought Toni home to meet her, a few weeks after he left the seminary, she displayed a very cold attitude, indicating a grudge for the women who, she believed, had taken her son away from a future in the priesthood and the fulfillment of her egocentric needs. She had her mind set, and no matter what Ray said, could change her belief that Ray and Toni had interfered in her plans for him. Ray, knowing that his mother could be impossible to please, was not willing to let her keep him away from a holiday with his father and sisters so he and Louise spent Thanksgiving ignoring his pouting mother.

On Christmas day, Ray stopped by his parent's house to offer them best wishes. His mother continued to pout, saying, "I can not understand how the one son I thought I could rely on, could let me down like you did. How could you turn away from God's calling?"

Knowing that trying to make his mother understand was like trying to get blood from a stone, Ray gave her a kiss on the cheek and said, "I hope that some day you will learn that there is more to life than what your neighbors think."

He walked to the living room, where his father was relaxing. "Merry Christmas dad," He said. I hope that mom will someday learn where to place her priorities, so I can feel comfortable coming to see you."

"Look son, I have been married to you mother for a long time, and I doubt that she will change now, so remember, no matter what she says or does, you are always welcome in this house."

"Thanks Dad." said Ray as he gave him a hug and departed for Toni's.

Chapter 13

Christmas and New Years went quickly. Ray was hired by Yellow Cab, and life was becoming very exciting for him and Toni. There was no question that they were seriously in love. Whitey was out of the picture, and Toni was now seriously thinking of what it would be like to settle into the family life with Ray. They spent as much time as possible together. Picnics, fishing, and going to professional baseball games took up most of their free time. They could hardly stand it when they were not together. It was obvious, that they would be getting married in the near future.

Ray had been working at Yellow Cab for about a year, when he decided it was time to spring the big question on Toni. He arranged to take her to dinner that weekend, at their favorite Sicilian restaurant.

He reserved a table by a window, where they could watch the people walk by, and try to guess what each one did for a living. They laughed a lot, and enjoyed the simple things of life, because they enjoyed each other so much. They often walked to their destination, and on occasion, they took a bus.

For a special occasion, they would take a cab. So when he arrived to pick her up, in a cab, Toni curiously said "A cab? This must be a very special occasion!"

"You will see!" he exclaimed. She was aware that they were going to their favorite Italian eating spot, but wondered what could be so special that Ray would pay for a cab, since money was not readily available for such things. She would later find out that the cost of the cab was paid by Ray's boss, because Ray had told him that he was going to propose.

The drive to the restaurant was brief, but for the couple in love, every minute together was full of excitement, as they sat in the back seat holding hands and talking about the day.

At the restaurant, they were greeted by Anthony, the owner, who had grown to love them like his own. They were taken to their table by Anthony's wife Sophie, an amorous full bodied middle aged lady who was always happy.

Ray and Toni enjoyed the couple very much, not only for their good Italian dishes, but for the love and joy they expressed to each other. It was an enjoyable and loving place to eat. No matter what the nationality, the customers were greeted with open arms and made to feel special.

Anthony was a very large and very strong man. He also had many relatives and friends of his blood, so a rude or insulting person was not tolerated in his restaurant. He politely invited those not tolerable to leave, and if they refused, they were physically removed. Only fools argued with Anthony.

Ray and Toni spent about two hours enjoying their dinner, while Anthony and Sophie flittered about like two love sick children.

They were already aware of Ray's intentions, and could not wait until he popped the question. They had prepared a special spumoni ice cream dessert for the occasion, and were anxiously waiting to bring it out. The bottle of wine that was served with dinner, was also a gift for the occasion, and not added to the bill, unknown to the loving couple.

Ray and Toni savored every bite of their meal, and played the passer by game while eating. They had no idea if what they guessed about the people walking by was correct, but they laughed a lot, and that was all that counted.

When they had finished, and their table was cleared, Ray reached across and grasped Toni's right hand with his left. "I've waited to ask you something for quite some time." he said, looking into her eyes. With his right hand, he then reached into his suit coat pocket, and pulled out a ring box. When she saw the box Toni smiled, as she anxiously waited for his question.

As he opened the box, and held it out for Toni to see a beautiful diamond ring, Ray asked, "Will you be my wife?"

Taking the ring and slipping it on her trembling finger, with tears in her eyes, Toni said, "Yes I will be proud to be your wife."

Anthony and Sophie had been watching from the Kitchen, and came running to the table with the colorful desert they were anxiously waiting to present. "Congratulations! Congratulations! We are so happy for you!" they expressed loudly. So loudly, that everyone else in the restaurant expressed their congratulations by applauding the couple. Ray raised his glass of wine to Anthony's customers, and thanked them.

In the days to come, they set a date, and made plans for a very nice wedding, even though they knew little assistance would come from their families.

They were married on June 10th 1932. The wedding was beautiful. Ray and Toni went beyond what the guests could have expected from a couple who were very limited financially. Tony wore a spectacular white gown draped with a veil that extended into a long train. She wore pearl white heels and carried a large bouquet of carnations and roses.

Ray wore a black and white tuxedo. His brother Dolor was the best man, and Toni's sister Agnes was the bridesmaid. The ceremony was held at the church they had been attending on Sundays. Ray's entire family was there, including his mother, who always had an irritating snobbishness about her. Toni's mom, sisters, and brothers all came, but as was expected, her father did not. Roland gave her away proudly.

They had a small but respectable reception, at which everyone was congenial, including Ray's mom for a change, much to his surprise.

Their honeymoon was celebrated at home in the apartment that they rented a month prior to the wedding. They had agreed on an inexpensive place to live for the next two years, so they could save to buy a home of their own. The apartment was small, but Toni, using her feminine touch, made it very comfortable. To herself, she practiced her new last name, Emond (E-mo-nd)

Chapter 14

Approximately two years into the marriage, believing that it was his place, to provide for his family, Ray asked, "Honey what do you think about quitting your job and staying at home?"

"You mean like a house wife? I would love to, but can we afford it?" she asked.

"I think so, I have taken a good look at our financial situation vs. my income, and we will even be able to save a little after our bills are paid."

"Well, if you would be happy with me at home, I will be happy to be there. It will give me a chance to make a nicer home for us." she said, as she gave Ray a kiss. To stay at home after working as a laborer since age 12 was like going on a long vacation. Washing dishes and cloths, sewing, and maintaining a home, was easy for her.

From that time on, Ray would go off to work, dressed in a gray or blue pin stripe suite, after Toni fixed him a nice breakfast, and kissed him goodbye. Toni would then go about doing the things necessary to make a home an enjoyable place to live. They made a great team, and they enjoyed life to the fullest. Even though they were budgeting to purchase a home, they made sure that there was always some money set aside for some of the fun things in life.

During the baseball season, they went to the ball games as often as they could. They enjoyed picnicking, fishing, and when it rained, an occasional musical. During the season, fishing was also an outlet for the tension that plagued Ray at the end of each month, when books had to be balanced, at work.

Toni also loved to fish. Once or twice a year, they made it a point to go fishing for striped bass at Narragansett beach, a popular resort on the Atlantic Coast in New England. They looked forward to the striper season when they could picnic on the beach, as they anxiously waited for a bite on the line that extended from their fishing rod, propped in the sand.

When the striped bass were running, baseball was out of the picture. This was a sport that Ray could physically participate in, and quite often be successful. He truly loved fishing. At the end of their day, they would have fun talking about the socialites they saw, and the fish that got away.

Occasionally, Ray would go fishing alone, because he wanted to fish around the tide changes, which made a day at the ocean very long. Toni would take that opportunity to catch up on some sewing and reading. On these days, Ray would walk out on the stone jetty, to the end, and cast as far as he could into the ocean.

He would time his arrival for low tide, so he could get all the way out on the jetty and remain through high tide, when the stripers came in close. This was very dangerous, since an extremely high tide could wash Ray from the jetty into the rough Atlantic, over a quarter mile from shore.

More than once, he found himself standing on an area, twenty feet in length by fifteen feet in width, surrounded by water, and would remain there until a tide change, one hour later. It was on one of those occasions, that Ray was hooked into a large fish, and in his excitement, failed to notice a ground swell, which ultimately swept him from the jetty. Luckily, he was an excellent swimmer, and made it to shore, but the fish got away and he lost his gear.

When he arrived home that day, Toni was at the door to greet him. "Where is your pole and fishing box?" she asked.

"It's a long story." Ray responded. That evening, he told her about the mishap, and tried to play it down by laughing, as he told the story.

Toni was upset, but would not ask the man she loved, to give up taking chances in the sport that he enjoyed so much. Quite often, on the days that Ray went out on the jetty, he would come home with one or two stripper bass between twenty and thirty pounds and act like a proud hunter fulfilling his duty to keep food on the families table.

Needless to say, Toni would prepare a meal with these offerings from the ocean that was fit for a king. Ray loved fresh fish, no matter how it was prepared and he always let her know how much he appreciated her cooking.

There were those days, that Ray came home empty handed, but the sound of the waves breaking on the beach, the crisp ocean air, and the anticipation of catching a big fish, allowed him to unwind, and get ready to face another week at his stressful job.

Toni worried about his stressful situation, and the effect it could have on his health, so seeing Ray come home from a fishing trip, in a relaxed state, and realizing how she had felt after a day doing the same, gave her reason to believe that this sport was good medicine for the both of them.

Chapter 15

The first year of marriage for Ray and Toni was as exciting as any couple in love could expect, but the peak of excitement came when Toni found out she was pregnant, and she saw how excited Ray became when she told him. He was so elated, that he insisted on celebrating over a fine dinner at their favorite restaurant. They had often talked about the excitement of raising a family, and now it was coming true.

Their next nine months were full of joy, as they discussed names and planned the baby's room. Ray treated Toni like a fragile piece of crystal and jumped to her every need.

It was June 1934, and the conclusion of her nine month term on a warm June evening. Ray and Toni were sitting in the living room listening to the radio when Toni suddenly rose up quickly from the sofa. "Oh! Oh! It's time!"

"Time for what?" asked Ray.

"It is time to get me to the hospital, before the baby is born in our living room!" announced Toni.

Anxiously taking her arm, Ray began leading Toni to the door. "Honey, get my suit case; it is by my dresser," said Toni.

"Let me take you to the car and come back for the case."

"No honey, I can get to the car by myself. Go and get the suit case. It will save time."

Ray nervously did as Toni suggested, and they went on as quickly as they could go to the hospital. On the way there, Toni laughed, as she told Ray how funny he looked, when she told him it was time, especially when he tripped and almost fell as he ran from the house to the car.

At the hospital, Toni said to Ray, as she laughed. "It's Ok to trip and fall now that you got me here. They might even give you a bed next to me, if you hurt yourself."

"Ha! Ha! I bet you won't be making wise cracks much longer." said Ray, and he was correct.

Shortly thereafter, Toni was admitted to a room, where she gave birth to a beautiful six pound girl, with a full head of shiny black hair. They named her Jenny and for the next two years, they loved and coddled her like there would be no others, but that was not to be for long.

In the month of May 1935, Toni gave birth to a healthy ten pound six ounce baby boy, and he was named Dolor after his uncle. Thus came a real period of adjustment. When Dolor reached the crawling stage, he got into everything and anything. Unless he was in the play pen, he had to be watched continually. He was a rough and tumble little guy, who brought a different kind of fun into the lives of Toni and Ray. Jenny was their little dress up doll, and Dolor made them laugh all the time that he was awake.

The two children brought them great pleasure, over the next three years. They were very proud of their son and daughter, and loved taking them on fun excursions.

Ray was doing well on his job, as the head accountant for the largest taxicab company in New England. They had two beautiful children, and were looking to buy a house. What more could a loving young couple want? How about another child?

In September of 1938, Toni gave birth to a seven pound boy, who they named Ronald. The nine months that she carried Ron, she was very ill, and quite often, thought she would lose this baby. She could not keep down her intake of food, and had to be placed on special injections.

The last three months of Toni's pregnancy, were spent in bed. Her sister Agnes looked after her, while Ray was at work. When Ray was at home, he made sure that he gave the children the attention that they required, and the rest of his time, was spent setting by Toni, trying to comfort her. "I wish that I could take on your discomfort, so you didn't have to suffer so," he would say, as he kept a cool cloth on her forehead, and comforted her until she fell asleep.

When the time came for Ronald to come into the world, the worst hurricane on record to hit New England was already causing havoc and devastation. The power was out in many areas, and travel was all but impossible. Toni had gone into labor about ten hours before the storm had struck, but had not left for the hospital, because her labor pains were inconsistent.

As Toni lay in her bed, her and Ray prayed that God would keep them safe, and allow this baby to be born at the hospital.

By the time she could be transported, twenty hours had passed since her first labor pain. In that time, New England's worst hurricane had uprooted much of the state of Rhode Island, but somehow, the hospital was spared. Thirteen hours after entering the hospital, Toni gave birth to her third child.

The baby seemed healthy, but she was just about at deaths door. Her doctor kept her in the hospital a few extra days, and told Ray to see that she stayed in bed at home for a week. He also advised Toni and Ray that this hurricane baby should be their last.

Chapter 16

Thanks to her strong constitution to live a full life, Toni got her strength back quickly, and that following year, they bought a cute three bedroom, two bath house called a Cape Coder. Other than Ron having developed severe Atopic Eczema on his upper torso, everyone was healthy and they felt blessed.

Like most young couples, life dealt out an occasional problem or two, but together, they faced everything head on. Ray's mother continued to be meddlesome, and Toni never heard from her father. But overall, their life ran relatively smooth, until the 3rd of March 1939, when Roland and Adie became the bearers of bad news. They drove out, to let Toni know, that her mom had suffered a severe stroke, the night before.

"Oh. God! How bad is she?" Toni asked, fighting back her tears.

"The doctor said she has lost her speech and her entire left side is paralyzed." said Roland.

"He also said It is too early to tell how much physical strength she will regain, if any." said Adie.

"So what you are saying is that mom could end up in a wheel chair for the rest of her life if she even survives this horrible affliction." responded Toni.

Placing his arm over his sister's shoulders Roland did his best to comfort her saying, "Let's not make any assumptions just yet. Mom is going to need a lot of support from all her children, especially since she won't get much from Pa. She will need, at least one of us by her side every day. Now more than ever, we need to show her how much we love her." Adie and Roland remained with Toni until Ray came home for work.

That evening, after the children were fed and settled in their beds, the four adults discussed what the best procedure for taking care of Emily would be when or if she left the hospital. They realized that a lot depended on how much of a recovery she made. They agreed that all of the children should give some assistance, when the time came.

That weekend, everyone got together out at the farm for a pot luck picnic, to arrange how the time with their mom would be divided up. Ovid was invited, but said he would leave the problem in their hands.

After almost two weeks in the hospital, Emily was discharged, showing very little improvement over the day she had entered. She could not talk, and would have to be in a wheel chair for the rest of her life. Fortunately, Toni's youngest brother and sister, Raymond age 18 and Minnie age 23, were still living on the farm so someone would always be there to help out. Everyone gave of their time generously, but Emily deteriorated rapidly over the next six months, and it wasn't long after that, Ovid concluded that his wife needed to be institutionalized. None of the children wanted this, but those who were living on their own were in no position to give more time to the situation.

It was September, when Emily was placed in a state institution, where she would have a nurse with her all of the time. Toni new this was best, but she took it very hard because her mother and Roland were the only one's who gave her the support she needed, when Ovid disowned her.

She made it a point to see her mother every week. She even took the three children, when the weather was good, and had them stand outside of the screened in area of the hospital where their Grandmother, generally setting in a rocking chair, could see them. Toni could not tell if her mother was able to recognize her or understand much of anything, but she believed that being there had meaning to her mom. The nurses informed Toni that she and Roland were the most consistent visitors. They had only seen her sisters a few times in eight weeks, and Ovid had not been by at all.

Toni had gone to visit her mom a few days before Christmas, and came home in tears. Seeing this, Ray asked "What is wrong honey? Is your mom Ok?"

"Oh! I just wish we had the room so mom could live here, and I could take care of her. Pa never visits her, and she is alone most of the time.

"I don't like the situation either, responded Ray. As soon as we can afford an addition to the house we will move her in with us."

"I sure do love you. You are always so thoughtful Toni responded," as she gave him a hug and a kiss.

Chapter 17

In the spring of 1940 the angel of death paid a visit to Toni and Ray. Life had been good, but that was about to change for reasons Toni will never understand. What was once a blissful happy life would now turn to painful anxiety?

They have been living in their neatly maintained home for almost two years. Ray's employer took a liking to him and showed his appreciation by giving Ray a considerable salary increase. The dreams of Toni and the man she loved so much were coming true.

They purchased a neat Cape Cod style house, white with black shutters and gables on the roof that frame the windows of the upstairs bedrooms. The garage is attached to the house, making it appear larger than it really is. The interior is well laid out, and Toni has decorated it nicely.

The first floor has a nice size living room with a red brick fireplace, a separate dinning area, kitchen, master bedroom and a bathroom. The upstairs consists of a bathroom and two nicely decorated bedrooms for the children. There is also a full basement.

In this house Toni and Ray planed to raise their children and hopefully live out their dreams. It is said that time heals all, and it appeared that Toni had put the days of being her father's bastard child and the trauma of her automobile accident behind her.

She and Ray were now well on their way to that story book

happiness which so many couples only dream of. Toni had no idea that she soon would be facing one of the most stressful times that a loving wife could face.

Ray had never been much of a complainer even though for sometime he had been suffering from severe abdominal discomfort that he only occasionally mentioned in a jovial manner. "I must have really upset the Lord today, because it feels like he just poked me in the stomach with a hot poker," he would say, with a chuckle.

Having spent close to four years in a seminary, Ray's sense of humor had developed around his biblical knowledge, vs. worldly beliefs. He believed that the jovial acceptance of his discomfort with prayer would be more beneficial to his health than complaining. He was well aware of his human weaknesses, and believed that allowing his self to be stressed over month end reports was the prime cause of his discomfort. The pain was always more acute at that time.

On a typical work day morning, Ray would enjoy a breakfast of two eggs, bacon and toast before leaving for work, but lately that had changed to just toast and coffee. He was obviously loosing weight, which gave Toni reason to be concerned.

"Honey, you are eating less and have lost quite a bit of weight, over the past month. I am getting worried!" She exclaimed!

"Oh don't worry sweetheart! Food just doesn't taste good to me right now. I'll get over it." he would respond.

Two weeks had elapsed since Toni had expressed her concern. Ray kissed Toni goodbye, and left for work, after eating only a piece of toast. Neither of them had any idea that the beginning of another very traumatic situation in their life, was about to unfold.

That afternoon, shortly after his lunch, which consisted of a corn beef sandwich and a coke, Ray developed a pain in his abdomen. He had returned to his desk, and had been working on the month end report for maybe twenty minutes, when he suddenly doubled over in pain.

With his arms folded around his abdomen, he remained in a slumped over position until the discomfort let up. When he was able to sit up, he felt as if he had a fever, so he went for some ice water. The receptionist noticed how pale he looked and asked if he felt Ok. "I think I ate a bad piece of corn beef and I think I had better go home. I will see you in the morning." Ray grabbed his top coat, picked up his brief case and departed.

"You are home early! Is everything Al right?" Toni asked.

"Oh, I must have eaten some bad corn beef at lunch, my stomach is killing me, and I think that I have a fever. I'm going to lie down for a while." Ray rested on their sofa, and went to bed early that evening without eating dinner. Toni was very concerned, and when he was still feeling poorly the next day, she insisted that he see a doctor.

That afternoon, Ray went to see their family physician, and was checked into the hospital that same day, to prepare for a lower gastro intestinal examination. The examination was completed the following morning, and it was determined that surgery was a priority.

Meeting with Toni and Ray in his office, the doctor said, "Ray's symptoms give me cause to be concerned, and I feel that an exploratory surgical procedure should be done immediately. There is no other way to tell if my suspicion is correct."

"Your suspicion, doctor? What are you saying?" Toni asked.

"I hope to rule out cancer." The doctor responded.

At that point, Toni wanted to cry, but for the sake of her husband, she held back her tears. "What can I do?" she asked, as she tried to maintain her composure.

"Well, you have about one hour to go home and gather up some items for Ray's stay in the hospital, before he is taken to surgery.

Before leaving the room, "I love you," Toni said as she gave Ray a kiss. I will be back as quick as I can."

The drive home seemed to take forever as Toni sobbed and thought of the potential outcome. "Why? Why, God?" she said out loud, as tears ran down her cheeks. "He is a good man. What did he ever do to deserve this?"

Arriving at the house Toni wiped her eyes and put on fresh lipstick so the children would not recognize that she was upset. Fortunately, they were still young enough that in their happy little minds, nothing appeared out of the ordinary.

After arranging for the children to be taken care of and gathering up some of Ray's personal items, Toni sped back to the hospital. She arrived just in time to give him a kiss and tell him she loved him before the orderly and a nurse took him to the operating room. She then went directly to the hospital chapel where she knelt for over an hour asking God to give her a sign that everything would be all right. She went, from the chapel to the lounge, where she continued to pray silently. She prayed for the strength to endure the worst if that was in God's plan for her husband.

The surgery took more than two hours and finally, Toni saw the surgeon coming toward her. By the sober look on his face, she knew that her perseverance was again going to be tested. Taking her by the hand, the doctor suggested that they walk to his office.

He assisted her to a chair and gave her a glass of water, as he said, "If at any time in your life, you will need to be strong mentally this is one of those times. With tears running down both cheeks, Toni stared at the doctor and listened intently...

"The surgery has revealed that Ray's lower intestine is almost entirely consumed by cancer, and it has spread to his liver. There is nothing we can do for him, other than make him as comfortable as possible."

"There must be something that can be done. He is only thirty-one years old." responded Toni.

"Believe me Toni, if there was anything that could be done, we would already be doing it. Medicine has not advanced enough yet, to deal with this severe of a situation. I am truly sorry."

"How long does he have to live?" Toni asked.

"His life expectancy is very limited. Three months, six months, maybe up to a year, but to be honest, I have no idea."

Toni's eyes filled with tears, and she began crying hysterically. With the help of the doctor, she soon gained her composure and asked to see Ray. She was taken to the recovery area, where she sat by his side and held his hand until he awoke from the anesthesia. He remained under heavy sedation for the next three days so there was very little communication between them.

On the fourth day, the doctor felt that Ray could be told of the findings. While Toni sat by the bed, holding Ray's hand, the doctor informed Ray that he had terminal cancer and his life expectancy was very short. Ray began to cry, as he looked into Toni's tear filled eyes. They wept in each others arms, for what seemed like an hour or more, before they were able to regain their composure. The rest of the day, they discussed how they would live out their remaining time together. They agreed that they needed to maintain a positive outlook, especially in front of the children, and to keep as active as Ray's condition would allow.

The next day, Toni was allowed to bring the children to see their dad. As they sat on his bed, next to him, Ray struggled to hold back the tears, knowing that it would not be long before he would never get to hold his children again.

Of the three children Jenny was the only one old enough to realize that something was wrong with her daddy, and in her precious little girl way, she said, "Don't worry Daddy! I will help mommy take care of you, until you are all better."

With that, Ray could feel the tears welling up in his eyes, so he asked Toni to get a nurse to take the children for a walk, so they wouldn't see him cry. That afternoon, he said good bye to the children, and did not see them until he was discharged four days later.

At home Ray felt quite a bit of discomfort, but the pain killers that the doctor had prescribed helped him to keep active with Toni and the kids. He resigned from his position at the Yellow Cab Co. and spent every possible moment with his family. They went to the beach as much as possible, and lay in the sun while the children played in the sand. In the evening they played with the children until their bed time.

Once the children were down for the night Ray and Toni would cuddle on the sofa, and talk of the day's activities. They would laugh about things the children did, and the fun they all had together. They tried to remain strong and positive, but that was not always possible. Quite often one or the other would break into tears before the evening was over.

Chapter 18

Ray had been home from the hospital about ten weeks when one afternoon while they were all out in the yard enjoying the warm sun, he complained that his pain seemed to be more frequent and more severe. "I think I need a stronger pain killer," he said. Lately, the pain seems to last longer, and I get tired more quickly, especially when I play with the children.

"I have been noticing the change, responded Toni. Did you tell the doctor on your last visit?"

"No, but you can bet that I will tomorrow." Ray answered.

The following day, Ray was put on morphine. The time that he and Toni had been dreading since he left the hospital, was closing in. Within three weeks Ray became bed ridden, and it was now a matter of days before he would pass on.

Each day for the next four days, Toni saw to it that the children where in Ray's view as much as possible, which he requested. On the fifth day it became obvious that the time was only hours away, so she helped each child up to give their dad a kiss for their last time. They were then taken to the living room, where they played with their toys.

Adie, Agnes, and Roland drove out this particular day to see how Ray and Toni were doing. After seeing how serious the situation had become, they remained and took care of the children until bed time so Toni could stay at Ray's side. Ray's parents, his sister Rita, and Ray had been stopping by each day and had arrived about two P.M.

It was very hard for mother and dad Emond to see their son, once a very healthy specimen of a man lying on his death bed so frail at such a young age. After briefly looking in and realizing that Ray no longer recognized anyone, they went out to the living room. Toni was left to be alone with her husband, who by now had gone into an unconscious state. She knelt by him, sobbing uncontrollably.

(Later, told by Toni in an interview). It was about five minutes before midnight, when a glow above the foot of Ray's bed caught Toni's attention. The room had been kept relatively dark except for a small light on the night stand, so this glow was strikingly noticeable. As she looked directly into what appeared to be a light of sparkling gold, a feeling of peace came over her, and from her lips came the words, "Mary Mother of God." She was witnessing the face of The Blessed Virgin looking down upon her and Ray.

From that moment, the anxiety that had been twisting up her insides was no longer there. Toni clutched her rosary tightly as she looked at Ray. He had a peaceful expression on his face, as if only sleeping, but he had passed on. Grasping Ray's hand in hers she wept, but no longer felt the anger that was within her before the light had appeared. After a few moments, Toni went into the living room and informed everyone that Ray had died peaceably. She did not mention the sighting.

It was getting late, and Roland had to get up early the following day so he gave his favorite sister a loving hug, and told her that he was leaving Aunt Adie to help out. Ray's family looked in on him one more time, gave Toni a hug, and left. "Louise and I will be by tomorrow," said Dolor, as they departed.

Knowing she would not be able to sleep, Toni asked Adie to make some coffee while she went to check on the children. The remainder of the night they sat and discussed the pitfalls of life, vs. the good side. They cried together, and agreed that without faith in a higher spirit they would be unable to make it through these hard times. It was about five AM when the both of them fell asleep where they were sitting.

At seven AM, Toni woke up and realized that the children would be opening their eyes soon. She quietly went and made herself presentable and then went to the children's room where they were just beginning to stir. She stood at the open door looking at them with tears in her eyes and said, "Thank you God for these three beautiful children who will always be a reminder of their wonderful father."

By the time the children were washed, dressed, and ready to eat Adie, had gotten up and began preparing breakfast. As usual, the two boys were hungry, but Jenny only nibbled on the delicious corn fritters their aunt had made special for them. Toni had no appetite, and left the kitchen to be alone.

After seeing to it that the kitchen was cleaned up and the children were playing in the living room, Adie went to check on Toni and found her crying by Ray's bed.

"Common sweetie you shouldn't be in here! This will only keep you depressed, and the children won't understand what is happening with their mother." You need to keep this door closed, until Ray's body is removed, so you can begin your recovery and so the children don't walk in. Common now let's go to the living room."

Toni wiped her eyes, and pulled the door behind her as she walked out. In the living room, the children played on the floor while Adie and Toni discussed the funeral preparation. Later that afternoon the men from the mortuary came to remove Ray's body, so Adie took the children for a walk to avoid having them see their daddy carried out.

The day went quickly, and while Adie was changing the sheets on Toni and Ray's bed, Toni was putting the children to sleep. She was not prepared to tell the children about Ray that evening and had planned to tell them in a day or two when she could be more in control of her own faculties.

Unfortunately, she had not planned on Jenny asking, "Mommy, can I go down and give daddy a good night kiss, and tell him I love him so he will feel better?"

At that moment, as her eyes filled with tears. Tony sat on the bed next to Jenny, put her arm around her, gasped and said, "Daddy has gone to be with God and he will no longer be coming home.

He will be watching over us from God's house."

"Why can't he still come home to see us sometimes?" asked Jenny.

"Because he will be very busy in heaven helping to prepare the way for us to join him there someday." responded Toni.

Seemingly satisfied with that explanation, Jenny kissed her mom and rolled on to her side as she said "I love you mommy."

Fighting back her tears, Toni said "I love you two honey." as she closed Jenny's door, and went down to the living room. Feeling exhausted, she wished Adie a good night, and said "I think that I will be able to sleep tonight."

In her room, Toni got down on her knees, focused her eyes on the crucifix above her bed, and with tears running down her cheeks, asked God for a sign that would let her know everything would be alright for her and the children. She had been on her knees for ten minutes or so when the same bright light that appeared just before Ray had passed on, manifested around the crucifix. Nodding her head and expressing thanks, Toni moved from her knees to her bed and soon fell fast asleep.

It was as if the weight of the world had been removed from her shoulders. To this day, if you asked Toni what had happened she would tell you that the Blessed Virgin had appeared to let her know everything would be alright for her and the children.

Ray's family assisted Toni in making the arrangements for his funeral, and Toni saw to it that the man she so loved was presented with all of the dignity he deserved. To this day, there stands in a well kept New England cemetery, an exquisite marble head stone bearing the chiseled in name of a man who was loved by a lady like many men only get to dream about.

Chapter 19

It wasn't long, when the often talked about In-law greed of many families, had begun to rear its ugly head on Toni's life.

Since childhood Toni's traumatic experiences made her a philosophical lady, and she now knew that she had to be strong for her children before anything else. She convinced herself that facing the future would be enough of a burden without dwelling on the past. Unfortunately, she could not anticipate what was about to happen only a few months after Ray had been placed in the ground.

Realizing that she was unable to keep up the house payments, Toni elected to try selling it so she could begin a new life for her and the children. She hadn't worked since she married Ray, and she knew that finding employment was not going to be easy, so the little profit that she would get on the sale could be helpful in her new beginning.

Toni had no sooner talked of selling the house, when Ray's mother came to her, saying "You can't raise the children and work too. Let me take them, and raise them properly like Ray would want."

"Thanks mother, but I will do just fine", responded Toni.

"Well, I don't agree. You are selling the children's home because you can't afford to live in it, and I suppose you will sell your self next."

Wanting to slap the meddling witch, Toni responded, "You may be Ray's mother, but I am the mother of his children, and I will be damn if you or anyone else will raise them, now leave my house and don't come back until you can show me the respect I deserve!"

"Well if you think this is the end you had better think again" responded Ray's mother as she stomped out the door.

Obviously, this situation did not set well with her. She still held a grudge against Toni for Ray having left the priesthood, and now Toni had faced her down over the children. This Catholic busy body was not going to sit still for this. She wanted to somehow get even with her son's widow.

Toni had been a widow for just over two months when she elected to go to their banker for advice on selling the house.

The branch manager, who had seemed so nice when Ray was alive, now reflected a different attitude. He was cold and calculating. Addressing her by her legal name, the banker said, "Emily why don't you let me make life easier for you. I understand that Ray had only a small life policy on himself therefore making it financially impossible for you to keep the house. Why don't you let us take the house back so that you will no longer have the burden of that payment. All you have to do is just sign these papers authorizing us to take the property over and you can get on with your life."

Toni knew exactly what was happening. Her mother-in-law and the banker attended the same church, and were quite often involved in the church affairs together. There was no telling what the two of them had discussed, but it obviously was not something that would be a benefit to her and the children.

Unnerved by the boldness of the banker she said, "I don't know what my mother in-law told you, but you can bet that I am a lot smarter than she or you realize. I do not appreciate your dishonest attempt to mislead me into giving up something we both know could eventually bring financial assistance to me and my children. If I were you I would go to confession now in fear that I might die in my sleep, and go directly to hell! What next?" she asked herself as she left the bank and drove to pick up the children at a friend's house. Little did she know that soon she would be facing another test of her endurance.

Turning into her driveway, Toni noticed a truck parked in front of the garage, and walking toward it were her mother and father-in-law, and Ray's sister each carrying a box of items in there arms. As she drove up and got out of the car, Ray's mother stood in defiance, but his father appearing as though he were embarrassed, looked toward the ground. Ray's dad wanted nothing to do with what was taking place, but he was just one of those men who found it hard to say no to his intimidating wife.

"What are you doing?" Toni asked.

"Now that Ray is gone, I thought it would be ok to come and get some things that I know he would have wanted us to have." Her mother-in-law responded, defiantly.

"Even If Ray did want you to have something you have no right to enter my home and remove it without my permission. Everything in there belongs to me and my children, and if there are some items that I decide we can live without, you will be the last to know about it. Now please take the things you carried out back into my house and leave this property! Pa I am surprised at you. Why do you let her do these things?" Toni asked.

He didn't respond. Ray's mother was frantic, but Toni knew that she would get over it, especially since she still wanted to see her grandchildren. Anyway, if she never did get over it, that would be no loss, thought Toni.

Less than two weeks went by, before the in laws stopped in unexpectedly. Ray's dad stood out by the curb while Toni met her mother-in-law at the front door. "What is it you want this time?" asked Toni.

"We have come by to ask if you would give Pa and me the money from Ray's life insurance policy. I know that he would want us to have it, especially since you will be getting a profit from the sale of the house. I also believe that he would want Pa to have the car."

"That's it, I have heard enough!" Toni responded as she glared at her mother in law. You are making a wrong assumption if you think I will be intimidated like you intimidate your husband. Ray and I agreed on how the estate will be settled, and until I decide what the children and I will need no one is getting a thing. You can bet that the life insurance and the car are two things that no one is going to get their hands on. Now, for the last time, Mother Emond! If you persist in trying to intimidate me I will sell what I don't want and you will get nothing."

Once again, Ray's mother was sent on her way empty handed. She had met her match in her attempt to intimidate Toni.

Chapter 20

In the following weeks Toni made arrangements to have the children taken care of at a nursery that was supervised by Catholic nuns. With the guidance of a good attorney, she kept the house on the market, and went searching for employment. She was a good organizer, and made use of every moment in the day.

Because of her limited education, Toni found her search for employment very disheartening. There were opportunities for her if she made herself available to some of the men doing the interviews. Putting these individuals in their place quickly, stifled her chances for what might have been a better form of employment than she would ultimately end up with.

After more than two weeks of job searching, Toni elected to accept an opening for a waitress at one of the finest hotels in Providence. There were no strings attached other than hard work, and her hours couldn't have worked out better relative to her children's schedule at the nursery. Toni soon became the lead waitress and was often requested to serve the lunches for the prominent businessmen who frequented the hotel and restaurant. Her tips reflected the appreciation of those she served and with that amount added to her hourly pay, she was able to take care of her obligations and save a few dollars.

The small savings account that Ray and Toni had opened a

few years prior to his death was depleted on medical and funeral expenses, so she knew how important it was to have some money to fall back on in an emergency.

The house had been on the market for about four months, when she finally received a reasonable offer. A Jewish man from out of the area really liked the house and the well-maintained neighborhood which was reflected by his offer. Toni's attorney recommended that she present the offer to the bank for a conclusion.

Thirty days later Toni received a letter advising her that the buyer did not qualify. Already aware that this man was self employed in a successful clothing store and that he should qualify easily, Toni concluded that the locals and their banker friend were attempting to keep a Jewish person out of the neighborhood. The Jewish people had always lived in a predominantly Jewish area and the ignorant wanted them to stay there.

Refusing to let the bank have their way Toni turned the matter over to her attorney, who gave the bank thirty days to substantiate why they refused the sale or a law suit was inevitable. Within two weeks of the attorney letter, the bank qualified the buyer and Toni sold her house making her financial situation less stressful. She made a profit of almost three thousand dollars which she was able to deposit in her small savings account.

When Toni's in-laws learned of the sale and that she would be moving soon, they were on her like bees on honey. Within one week of the completed sale, Ray's mother showed up at Toni's doorstep seeking freebies. "I understand that you have sold the house and made a nice little profit for yourself." she said, with an affectionate guise. Don't you think that Ray would want Pa and me to have some of the furnishings and other items, now that you have some money?"

"Hmm! Mother Emond, you and that banker must be friendlier than I thought. He must have been in contact with you immediately after the financial transaction was finalized."

"Well! I happened to see him in church last Sunday, and out of my concern for you and the children, I asked if he knew how the sale was going. He only told me what he knew and nothing more."

"Oh! And are you here asking to take home some of the

furnishings, because of your concern for me and the children? Let me try to make it as clear as possible, mother Emond! If you wish to come and visit the children before we move away you are welcome to stop bye most any time, but if you come with the intention of asking me to give you some of our personal things, don't bother to stop."

Chapter 21

For the next three weeks, Toni spent almost every evening after work, looking for a small house or an apartment. Most everything available was owned by snooty New England Yankees. Over and over she was told, "We do not rent to widows with children." or "We do not rent to the dirty French."

With less than a week left to find a home, Toni even considered living in a tent before resorting to the one thing she desperately wanted to avoid, which was calling on her father for help. She knew that her sisters and brothers had their own problems, and did not need the headache of a guest with three children, and that Ovid had moved into a large three bedroom section of a Victorian house that had been remodeled into a two family dwelling.

With only five days to vacate her house, Toni picked up the telephone. Grasping the receiver tightly in her trembling hand, "Operator, will you please place a call to Ovid Paulhus at #......." Anticipating the voice from hell, the voice of the man she called her father, the man who denied her as his daughter, Toni's heart pounded out of control.

"Hello!" came a deep unpleasant greeting.

"Pa it is Antoinette!" she said in a soft trembling voice.

"What do you want?" came Ovid's response in a tone that was colder than an ice storm in February.

Instantly, like so many other times in her young life, Toni felt that heart wrenching feeling of being unwanted come over her. Trembling and unable to speak she hung up the receiver and walked to her car where she sat for a few moments in prayer, asking God for the strength to hurdle those obstacles in her life for which there seemed no retort. Telling herself "Tomorrow is another day," she started her vehicle and drove to pick her children at the nursery.

At five the next morning, Toni was awake and preparing for another day. After seeing to her children's needs, she drove them to the nursery and then on to her job. Throughout her day, she would recall the incident with her father, but her strong character kept her on track until her shift was over.

She was on her way to pick up the children, when a voice in her head told her that she should call Ovid back and she should remain strong. That evening Toni took a philosophical view of her situation and decided that she would call Ovid from her place of employment in the morning. 10:45 A.M., a slack time for the restaurant, Toni went to the telephone and asked the operator to ring her father's number.

As she held on for an answer, one side of her was hoping that he would not be home, and the other was telling her that she needed to have closure with Pa, so she could get on with the rest of her life.

He was at home and after a moment or two, from the telephone receiver came a bellowing "Hello!"

"Pa, it is Antoinette again. I apologize for hanging up on you yesterday, but your tone frightened me."

"Frightened you? What the hell are you talking about? If you have something to say, say it or don't waste my time."

"Pa, I am calling to ask for your help! The children and I need a place to live and we have only three more days that we can stay at the house, because it has been sold."

"Why in the hell haven't you started looking for a place before now? What makes you think that I would want a woman with three kids living with me?"

"I have been looking for a place for over three weeks, Pa! No one with a clean unit will rent to a widow with children, and some landlords, have even said they don't rent to us dirty French people. We only need a place to stay for a few weeks, until I can find something that will make a good home for the children!"

"Dirty French, who in the hell called you that?"

"The Payettes in that big house down the road a way from where you live? I thought they were friends of yours!" Toni exclaimed.

"Those damn Yankees? They're no friends of mine! As far as I am concerned, they have always been a greedy bunch of bastards, and I want nothing to do with them. Anyway, how long did you say you will need to be here if I agree to let you move in?"

It seemed as if Ovid was having a change of heart. Was it because those Yankees had referred to his nationality as being dirt? "A month at the most by then I should have found something suitable for me and the children." Tony said enthusiastically.

"Ok, but remember, you will be responsible for your share of the expenses, just like renting an apartment."

"Thank you Pa! If it is all right with you, I will bring a few things to your place this evening, and we can talk more.

"Yah, Ok! I suppose that will be a good idea. I will be done with my dinner about 6:30 so come around 7:00."

Aware that her father was going to be very hard to live with, she still felt as if a very heavy burden had been lifted from her shoulders. Now the children would at least have a safe place to live until she could find something better.

Toni had visited her father's place, once before, when she had driven out with Ray, shortly after Jenny was born. She knew that he had plenty of room, but he was still living twenty years behind the time. Ovid's house was heated by wood in an old iron stove in the kitchen and oil stove in the living room. The upstairs bedrooms were without heat except for a small single burner kerosene stove that was placed at the top of the staircase, only on cold winter nights.

The house did not have a furnace, because of the miserly builder and owner T.K. Windsor who was a friend of Ovid. There was no inside plumbing except for a hand pump to get water to the kitchen sink. When it became necessary for a family member or guest to relieve themselves, the outhouse was situated about eighty feet out the back door. All foods that had to be kept cold were placed in a wooden icebox, for which ice was obtained every third day, from a traveling iceman. Ovid did not seem interested in the finer things of life. Keeping up with progress, was not a top priority for him.

That evening at Ovid's house, Toni nervously discussed when she would start moving her things in. "My new appliances especially the refrigerator, will make life a little easier for all of us." she said, expecting her father to appreciate the suggestion.

"I don't want your appliances because they cost too God-damn much to operate! I have done just fine without any of those new gadgets that you women can't seem to get along without."

"But Pa, in the long run it will be less costly to have a refrigerator because the perishable food will last longer and you will no longer have to purchase ice." Toni said, attempting to reason with him.

Ovid liked to eat, and the thought of being able to keep more food in the house caused him to consider what Toni had so wisely presented. "Let me think about it and I will let you know tomorrow. If I do agree, it will be with a stipulation that the refrigerator and your lighting fixtures, which are needed, will be the only electrical items that you will bring to this house."

Relieved by the thought she would be able to bring the refrigerator and her lamps, especially two crystal bed side lights that were a gift to her and Ray from aunt Adie, Toni did not press the subject any further. After putting the clothing and a few other items, she had brought with her into the room that would be hers; Toni expressed her thanks, and departed.

To avoid the cost of a mover, Toni asked her brother in-law if he and some of the family would assist in transporting hers and the children's things to Ovid's house that Saturday.

In the meantime, she would also move some things in her car after work, not only to help with the load, but also to ease up some of the tension with her father before the actual move in.

On the last visit with the children Toni still felt her father's coldness, so she hoped a few more visits prior to the actual move in might give him a chance to loosen up a little. Arriving after his dinner was the safest, but she had to be sure that she recognized when it was time to leave, which was made known to her when he would pick up a Zane Gray western and start reading in her presents.

That Thursday and Friday, while Toni was transporting some

items, after work, she witnessed what appeared to be a softer side of her father, as the children sat by him and listened to his stories about growing up. Ron, the baby, wasn't much interested, but Jenny and Dolor seemed to be fascinated with the stories which were slightly influenced with a page or two straight out of one of his Zane Gray books.

Chapter 22

The Move did not go as smoothly as she had hoped. As Toni's in-laws are helping to load the truck, she notices that her things are being handled rather roughly.

"I really appreciate the fact that you have taken the time to help me and the children, but I wish that you would all try to be a little more careful with our things." Toni said with a slight smile.

Disappointed that she could not have the items she was so sure would be hers, Mother Emond rudely responded, "If it seems we are being too rough with your things, you can always get someone else to do the job, as we have other things that we would rather be doing."

"I apologize, mother Emond. I appreciate all of the help, and I will try to be less critical." Toni said, as she struggled to maintain her composure. Once everything was loaded Toni secured the house and asked her in-laws to go on ahead while she stopped by the bank to turn over the house keys, and sign one more paper, which took about fifteen minutes. From the bank, Toni made a short stop at the market for a few groceries, and then drove to meet her In-laws who she thought would be waiting at her father's place.

When she got to within eye sight of the house, Toni said to Jenny, "I don't see the truck, I wonder if they got lost?" But when she turned into the driveway that led to the back of the house, what she saw took her breath away. Her in-laws had been there and gone, and all of her furnishings, along with the children's toys, and boxes of goods were in a pile on the ground. It appeared as though the items weren't even set there with care but just thrown.

Toni got out of the car, and as she looked over the pile she found that several things were damaged, including the children's toys. "Why? Why? What have I done to deserve this?" she cried out.

Ovid arrived home about twenty minutes after Toni had gotten there. "What in the hell is this?" he asked, looking at the heap of household goods, and then at the children sitting on the back steps with their mother, who was in tears.

"Ray's family did this. They couldn't wait until I arrived to let them in. I knew his mother didn't like me, but how could they do this to the children?"

"Just one more example, as to why I like animals more than people. Common, let's all work together, and get these things into the house, before it gets dark." Ovid said, in a sympathetic tone. Even Ronnie who was less than two, carried in a few toys.

That evening, after making the children comfortable and thanking her father, Toni got down on her knees and thanked God for giving her and the children a warm and safe place to live. She also prayed for continued strength to carry on.

Aware that life in a poison ivy patch would probably be less stressful than living with the man who refused to claim her as his daughter, Toni vowed to do whatever it took to keep peace.

Even though Ovid had shown that he disliked the mistreatment of Toni and the children by her in-laws, his empathy was only for that moment, and he was not about to change his methods. Toni was once again under his roof, and she would be better off to never question his demands. The fact that she had to get up an hour earlier each morning for the longer drive to the nursery and her work, meant to Ovid that he could take advantage of that situation.

Toni and the children had been settled in her father's house, only a week, when she was told, "Since you will be getting up before I do each morning you may as well prepare my breakfast, and I will eat with you and the kids."

"But Pa, I will be rushing to get myself and the children ready so I can be at work on time. Anyway, the children only eat cream of wheat or oatmeal."

"I don't see a problem with that! You can fix me bacon, eggs and toast at the same time," responded Ovid. I will be ready to eat just about the time that you are feeding them. Realizing that it would be futile to dispute what her father wanted, Toni agreed to his demand and went to her room.

When ever Toni would arrive home, Ovid would be sitting by the wood stove in his over-sized chair reading Zane Gray and had obviously done nothing to assist in the preparation of dinner, nor had he even set the table. There were occasions when she would walk in with tired and cranky children, and Ovid would ask, "How long will I have to wait before my dinner is on the table?" Concern for the children was minimal. As far as he was concerned they were not of his blood, so he dealt with them on that level.

Quite often, Toni wanted to speak out to her father about his uninspiring attitude, but feeling obligated and fearing a reprisal, she controlled her tongue and did what was demanded of her, until one day when she had to work a large business luncheon which caused her to leave work an hour later then usual.

That day, after picking up the children, Toni decided to stop at Charlie's Diner for supper so the children wouldn't be eating after their bedtime. They arrived home a few minutes before seven P.M. to find Ovid sitting in his usual spot. "Where the hell have you been? he bellowed. I expect my dinner on the table by five thirty, at the latest."

"I worked later than usual Pa, so rather than having the children eat too late, I took them out for dinner.

"And what am I supposed to do for my dinner, wait until you get home at this hour?"

"I thought that you would go ahead and fix yourself something, once I had not arrived by five-thirty"

Expecting an apology and not hearing what he wanted to hear, Ovid blurted out, "You're an unfit mother. I took you in for the sake of the children, and this is the appreciation you show for it!"

He would brow beat her until she was in tears, and even then he did not let up, until she would bundle up the children and leave, often driving the dark country roads, or visiting her Aunt Adie until she was sure that he was in bed asleep before going home.

There were times that the children were already in bed asleep, and Ovid would begin his browbeating, so to maintain her sanity, Toni would go to her car and drive to a tranquil place where she could reflect on the life she was living. There, she often concluded that she was luckier than many, and that God still had a plan for her. Sometimes she would go to a movie, where she would cry herself to sleep, and be awakened by the usher at closing time. By the time she arrived home, she would have thanked God for the strength to face up to the unpleasant things in life.

Chapter 23

After fifteen months, and still unable to find a decent place to rent for her and the children, life with father did not get any easier. But as time went on, little changes such as new employment close to home, and enrolling the children in a near by catholic school, helped to ease some of Toni's tension. Jenny was now in the second grade, and Dolor in Kindergarten. Ronnie, age 4, was cared for by the nuns at the school nursery, and all three were transported by a bus.

Toni now had almost one hour extra each morning and time to fix her father a nice breakfast, without feeling rushed. This helped to release some of the early morning tension with Ovid.

While Toni was working a business lunch at the hotel, she overheard that the Textron Corporation had openings for assembly line workers, and the starting pay was more than she was earning, including her tips. She wasted no time applying for the position, and was hired to be a part of the growing female work force brought on by the anticipation that the U.S. would be going to war, since President Roosevelt was doing his best to get the United States involved for the sake of the profiteering corporations.

The Textron Corporation, like many other industries of that era, was gearing up to manufacture defense products for the strong possibility that the United States would be drawn into a war which could have been avoided by minding our own business.

Germany had a new Fuhrer by the name of Adolph Hitler, a moron who after his appointment to the chancellorship in 1933, by the Elite Fascist's, developed a strong appetite for world power. He not only wanted to rule all of Europe, but also believed that he could eventually eliminate all Semites, and create the perfect human race through his doctors and scientists. The race would be made up of only blond-hair and blue eyed men and women.

By 1941, Hitler's Nazi's annihilated no less than one hundred and twenty thousand Jews and his threat continued. Thus the gearing up of industry to develop defense items for a war against Germany, began. The role of the female in the work world changed dramatically. Women entered the work force in record numbers, and ultimately, there came the title, "Rosie the Riveter." which depicted a strong-arm female laborer representing all women working for freedom.

By 1944, the American factories that had in prior years, only produced a low number of aircraft, had now produced over 90,000 planes for combat including the infamous Flying Fortress.

There were a total of 250,000 planes built for WWII. In 1940, the U.S. army was made up of only 175,000, poorly equipped soldiers, but by 1945, the military had grown to 8 million personnel, and was equipped better than any other army in the world.

Prior to WWII, many of the young American citizens grew up thinking cynically of patriotism because of the false economy and degrading depression of the 1930's. The war changed that thinking to a teamwork mentality. The hardships of rationing food, no tires, no production of automobiles, other than for the military, no appliances, and living three families to an apartment, was taken in stride by the American people. They felt that life would be better when the war was over.

Toni, like so many young mothers, had become a Rosie the Riveter, and was proud of it because, like most patriots at the time, she believed that this war was necessary for the protection of America. Her job at the Textron Corporation was to braid nylon into one hundred foot long, by one-inch diameter climbing ropes. The American soldier used the ropes to scale walls and high cliffs, like the cliffs at Normandy beach, during the famous 1944, World

War II European invasion. Each rope had to withstand a stress test of eight hundred to a thousand pounds, before it was released to the military.

It wasn't long before Toni became a department instructor, on the building of these ropes, and from there was promoted to the lab of the parachute division where she was responsible for the testing of materials used in the manufacture of the parachutes. This position gave her an increase in pay, but created the complication of having to take a train, from Providence, Rhode Island to Boston, Massachusetts, thereby causing her to arrive home later in the day, and having less time with the children.

Ovid, also working more hours at the Bleachery, on a military contract, still coerced Toni, as if she were his maid, even though she would often be exhausted from her long days. He did very little, if anything, to help make her life less hectic. When he arrived home from work, he would do only what was absolutely necessary at that moment, like stocking the wood stove, so he would be warm in the winter, or filling the kerosene tank on the cooking stove, so that it was ready for Toni to make dinner. His personal comfort was the priority.

Jenny and the two boys would already be home from school, so Ovid would at least see that they were safely playing, after Jenny had set the table, and Dolor brought in wood and dumped the trash. When Toni would arrive, sometimes after seven PM, she would find Pa sitting in his chair reading, and the children waiting for dinner.

Finally frustrated enough to speak out, after arriving home late one evening, and finding that her father didn't even have the compassion to at least give the children a snack, Toni threw down her coat, glared at Ovid and said, "I don't know what you did before I moved in Pa, and I really don't care, but anyone who will sit and let children, who are incapable of fixing there own dinner, go without, at least a glass of milk, is a real bastard! If it wasn't for the children, there would be no dinner tonight, and you could fix your own or go without."

"I told you when you asked to move here, that you would be expected to prepare my meals, along with the kids, and that is what I expect, or you can move out."

"If I could find a safe place for the children, you can bet I would move tomorrow!" Toni said, as tears ran down her cheeks, and she went on to prepare dinner.

That night, Ovid made it a point to be verbally abusive to Toni in front of the children, at the dinner table. "Grandpa, why are you so mean to my mother?" Little Dolor asked.

"Be quiet and mind your business, or I will send you from the table, and you won't eat."

"Yes honey, you are still too young to question your grandpa, no matter how rude he talks to me, so please eat your dinner quietly." said Toni, in a loving tone.

After dinner, the children spent a few loving moments with their mom as she explained how lucky they all are, even if Grandpa is grumpy.

Roland had kept in contact with his favorite sister from the time that she had moved from the farm to their aunt Adie's, and more often, after she moved in with her father. Toni saw her younger brother Ray, only occasionally, prior to moving to Ovid's place, but from that time on they too became close, and on more than one occasion, one or the other of her brothers, told their father he needed to slack off on his demands of her. That helped for a short time, but soon Ovid would go back to his old ways.

On Sunday's, when her brothers would occasionally come by, Toni would fix a special meal after which they would all sit in the living room and play games, or go out in the front yard if the weather permitted. They treated Dolor and Ronnie like their own, which was important to her, and showed equal love for Jenny, but after all, she was a little girl, and could not be treated rough like the boys. Her brothers, both tall and well built were very special to her, but soon they would be a great distance apart.

Chapter 24

On December 7th, 1941, to the astonishment of all of America, the Japanese, who had been wagering war in the Pacific since 1940, made an early morning bombing attack on the U.S. Base at Pearl Harbor, Hawaii, sinking naval ships, and killing 2300 American military personnel. It was an attack that could have been avoided had President Roosevelt and his Secretary of State, Cordell Hull agreed with the plan for peace presented to the State Department by a group of citizens from both Japan and China.

Both Roosevelt and Hull turned down a ninety day truce offering during which Japan and the United States could have arrived at a peaceful settlement. On November the 26th, Hull tossed away the truce offering and issued an ultimatum to the Japanese which they refused.

On December 8th, President Roosevelt declared war against Japan, and on December 11th, the U.S, joined Great Britain against Germany and Italy, who had declared war against Poland, Britain and France. World War II was under way, and Toni's proximity, in relationship to her brothers, would soon go from a few miles, to thousands of miles apart. It wasn't long after war had been declared that Roland, who loved the ocean, joined the Navy and after boot training, was assigned to a destroyer, (Battle Ship) and sent to the Pacific Fleet.

Ray who had been working as a carpenter joined a Navy team called the Sea Bees. These were the men who, after the Marines had taken over a strategic area in the Pacific, would go in and construct an air strip, build living quarters for the soldiers stationed there, and build bridges to bring in equipment and supplies. The Sea Bees faced the same dangers as any other combat unit because quite often the Japanese would return to try and take back the zone they were driven from. Many men were wounded or killed while working on a construction project until larger companies of Marines were stationed as fighting support while the Sea Bees completed their assignment.

Both of Toni's brothers were at war in the Pacific, yet they still managed to write an occasional letter to her or their father, to let them know that they were ok. Roland had experienced off shore combat when his ship fired on Japanese gun batteries that were dug into the hills of Pacific Islands, and had fired on the US Marines landing on those islands. Raymond was trying to keep from getting shot by snipers as he worked on the construction of strategic projects. Even Ovid's tough exterior would allow his concern for his sons to show through whenever he received a letter.

Hanging in the window next to Ovid's chair, was a red, white and blue shield with two white stars which signified that he had two sons fighting in the Pacific. Glancing at the shield he would make comments like, "I know the boys can take care of themselves, but I will be glad when the Japs are forced to surrender, and my sons can come home."

In response, Toni would say "I will continue to pray every day that God will keep them safe, and send them home soon." Unfortunately, the Pacific and European wars continued to escalate, and Toni would not be seeing her brothers for quite a long time.

As the war escalated, more hours at work were demanded because there was a need for more equipment and supplies. Her father showed signs of mellowing out a little, but he still expected her to do more than her share. Fortunately, the children were in school all day, and then bussed home where Jeannine saw to it that they were safely in the house until Ovid arrived. The war years were tough on a widow with children. Each day the children needed love and understanding no matter how tired mom got. Sometimes that love required a strong disciplinarian, which Toni learned shortly after becoming a widow.

While still in the hospital, after the birth of Jenny, Toni's doctor told her, "Now that you are a mother I want you to remember that you can avoid many of the worries that come with having children if you are willing to be lovingly firm until they reach age six. A smack on the bottom or their hand, when they knowingly break your rules will teach them respect for you and themselves. If you don't raise them with discipline by age six they will be hard to control, and you can only try guiding them from that point, which could lead to disappointment."

Between the obligation of being a first rate mom, a good employee, and keeping up with the demands of her father, Toni had very little time alone. She was lucky if she managed to get out by herself for a movie or a short Saturday evening ride, once in a two week period. This was generally only done out of desperation after being brow beat by Ovid. On occasion, she would go off to be alone, to think out all of the stress that comes to a widowed mother with two brothers off at war, and a patriarch father.

To Toni, God was her best friend. She believed that he would never let her down. When she felt the stress was getting to her, she would turn it over to God, through prayer. She would often say "Lord please give me the strength to carry on, as you would have me, under the circumstances."

After praying, she often felt as if her perseverance had been refueled and she could continue to face any dilemma that may crop up unexpectedly. Sunday was always good for her, not only from going to church, but also from the exhilarating energy that manifested within her after being with her children all day. Even Ovid believed in respecting the Sabbath, though he didn't feel it had to be done in a church.

When Jenny and Dolor. asked why he did not go to church, he courteously said, "All Christian religions teach that the Ten Commandments are the laws of God. It is not against his laws for a person to worship him from home, and that is why I do not go to church."

The children seemed satisfied with his answer, even though they had not learned the Commandments yet. No one had ever heard Ovid praying, but it was known that he sent money to a church every week. He obviously believed, but to what extent no one knew.

Toni's brothers have been gone over a year and a half, and though she still worries for them, life with Ovid has been less stressful since he seems to have mellowed out some.

Unfortunately, the dark cloud that seemed to have left Toni, is about to return.

Chapter 25

It is summer vacation for the children, and a beautiful, Saturday morning. Toni is at work, and the three kids are happily playing a game of tag out by the old barn when suddenly, Dolor sets down on the ground, and covers his eyes. "Why are you doing that? asked Jenny. We aren't playing hide and seek,"

"I feel funny. My head is hot, and everything is going round and round. Oh...Oh! I am going to throw up."

As Dolor up chucked his breakfast, Ronnie stood and watched in wonderment, and Jenny ran to tell her Grandpa.

"Grandpa! Grandpa! There is something wrong with Dolor. He just sat down and threw up."

"Well let's go see what his problem is. Ovid and Jenny walk to where Dolor is still setting. What's the problem boy?"

"I feel real funny Grandpa. Everything is spinning and I can't get up."

"Here let me feel your forehead. Yup! You have a fever!" Ovid exclaimed picking Raymond up and carrying him to the house. We had better get you into bed, and call the doctor." said Ovid.

The doctor arrived within the hour, and after checking Dolor's symptoms for related illnesses, he informed Ovid that his grandson appeared to have Scarlet Fever.

"I will be able to give you a definite answer tomorrow, after his urine specimen has been evaluated. I have given him penicillin to fight the virus, and aspirin to get his temperature down. I doubt that he will want to eat much, so tell his mother to be sure to at least feed him Jell-O, and keep plenty of cold fluids in him."

It was after two o'clock in the afternoon by the time the doctor had departed. Toni would arrive home around five, so Ovid decided not to call her at work and make her worry. When she did arrive, and learned of the situation, she became extremely concerned. This virus, known for its high fevers, could cause severe brain damage, and even death. Dolor's fever was holding steady at 104.5, and he was delirious.

Toni did not go to work the next day and by ten o'clock that morning, the doctor confirmed that Dolor had an advanced case of Scarlet Fever. The house was quarantined, and a notice was placed on their door advising visitors to stay away. The family was confined to the house for the duration of the sickness.

For the next two days, Toni remained by Dolor's side, occasionally wiping his forehead and asking God not to take him from her.

Seeing Dolor lying there in such a state, caused Toni to recall the loss of Raymond Sr., which made her very melancholy.

Within a few days, Dolor's temperature had dropped to within the safe zone, but not before the sickness was passed on to Ronnie. Fortunately, because of an early diagnosis, only two days after Dolor's full recovery Ronnie's temperature dropped close to normal, and soon the quarantine on their home was removed. Toni was able to return to work as was her father who is now only working part time, because of his age.

By the time the war was nearing its second year, the letters from Raymond, had stopped. Letters were still received from Roland, who had also lost contact after Raymond had been sent to the Philippines. Even Ovid was becoming concerned. For all they knew, Raymond was dead.

"I refuse to believe that Raymond is not still alive." stated Ovid. He is smart and has a lot of common sense . I know that he will be coming home one day."

Toni could tell that her father was very concerned, because he was getting back to being his old grumpy self again, demanding that she and the children cater to his wants, which could be unrealistic at times.

After all, Raymond was his baby, and had a personality that pleased his father, unlike Roland, a Libra who had an innate need to want balance in his life, which often got him in trouble.

Chapter 26

In January of 1942 Raymond's company of Sea Bees was ordered to the island of Bataan in the Philippine Islands. The armies under the command of Gen. Mac Arthur, had established this as a strategic battle area, and the Sea Bees were assigned to build an air strip so the American planes would be closer in striking distance to the enemy.

In April of 42, Bataan was attacked and overtaken by the Japanese. The American soldier's who had survived the battle, were taken prisoner and placed in a concentration camp, on the island. The inhumanities that these soldiers were subjected to were in complete violation of the Geneva Convention, which all warring countries, except Japan, had agreed to.

Each day except Sundays, the prisoners were marched two by two, from the camp to a work site. Those Soldiers, American and British, who were too weak to complete the march, were shot and pushed from the trail, their bodies left for the animals and insects. Hundreds of soldiers were killed in what was later called "The Bataan Death March."

It was March of 1943. Raymond had been a prisoner for almost a year, and had been subjected to beatings which left his back permanently scared, dunked upside down in a barrel of human waste, leaving him with tuberculosis and was fed only a bowl of cold rice once a day. He had gone from over two hundred pounds down to ninety-eight pounds and his system had succumbed to Malaria. He had been forced to march on Saturday, and was barely able to stand after returning from the grueling march to and from a work site, where the prisoners were forced to labor in the hot and very humid jungle. It was doubtful that he would complete the next march on Monday. That Sunday, Raymond remained in his cart and forced down the cold rice in an attempt to gain his strength back.

It was a warm tropical Monday morning in March of 1943, when the guards forced the prisoners from their shanties, and the ritual began. The prisoners had walked about a mile and a half when Raymond's legs began to buckle under and he fell to his knees. Before he was able to stand he felt a blow to his back, from the butt of a Japanese guard's rifle, causing him to fall over onto his side. The guard then kicked him and ordered him to get up, but no matter how he tried, Raymond was too weak.

Realizing that at any moment he would be shot and left in the swamp grass along the side of the trail, he could only close his eyes and wait. Suddenly there was the loud burst from the guard's rifle, and an instantaneous burning of his flesh, as a bullet traveled through his back near the left shoulder blade, and out his chest, below the heart. Raymond could feel the tip of the guard's gun barrel poking at him, to determine if he were dead. Satisfied that Raymond was dead, the guard pushed him from the trail and into the swamp grass.

In extreme pain, and able to hear his heart pounding loudly in his head, he laid there on his back quietly and totally still, until the sound of the guards giving orders could no longer be heard. The guard had failed to kill him, and now was his chance to escape he thought to himself, but how far could he get? He did not have the strength to even get to his knees, and there was a chance that he would bleed to death, from the wound.

Dragging himself through the snake-infested swamp in waist high grass, pulling with his elbows, and pushing with his toes, Raymond clung to the mere possibility that he might find Philippine guerilla troops who he had heard were in the area fighting on the side of the Americans.

He dragged himself through the swamp land for what seemed like hours, before passing out from the pain and loss of blood.

When he awoke three days later, he found himself lying on a cart in a shanty with a man who appeared to be an officer, looking down at him. Raymond feared that he had been captured again.

"Good to see you are going to live," said the soldier, in his thick Philippine accent.

"What is this place? How did I get here? Are you one of the Gorillas I have heard about?" asked Raymond.

"This place is where we hide from the Japs before and after we pull a raid on them, when they are out on patrol. You were carried here by some of my men after they found you passed out in the swamp, and yes to your last question. You might say I am the gorilla in charge."

Raymond remained in the care of these brave allied troops until Gen. Mac Arthur returned with his forces, in the spring of 1944, and forced the Japanese to give up the islands.

Chapter 27

Back in Greenville, Rhode Island, in the fall of 1943 Ovid had received a letter from the U.S. Defense Dept. advising him that Raymond was reported missing in action. The letter went on to explain that he may be a prisoner of war on the Island of Bataan which was in the control of the Japanese Imperial Army.

The defense dept. expressed their sympathy, and wrote that they would keep Ovid informed of any information they receive about his son.

Toni arrived home early the day that the letter had been received. Ironically, Raymond had been on her mind most of the day. "I have been thinking about Raymond quite a bit today. I hope he is all right." she said to Ovid, as she entered the kitchen to begin preparing dinner.

"Coincidentally!" exclaimed Ovid. I received a letter from the Department of Defense this morning. It says that they think Raymond is a prisoner on the Island of Bataan in the South Pacific.

"OH God! There is no telling what he must be going through. Some of the ladies I work with have brothers and husbands in the Pacific and they say the Japs are ruthless, according to the letters they receive. I am going to church after dinner to pray that God will bring him through this terrible ordeal. Thank God Roland is still sending us letters. I don't know what I would do if they were both captured."

For the next four months, Toni or her father would anxiously go for the mail each day expecting to receive something from the Department of Defense.

They had received letters from Roland, who was also very apprehensive about his brother's situation, but nothing from the government. Then, one day in February, Ovid read the headline, "Mac Arthur's Troops Take Back Bataan and Free American Prisoners".

Toni also heard the news at work and rushed home to see if her father had learned anything about Raymond. Unfortunately, there was nothing in the mail, but they could now at least anticipate he would be coming home soon.

After the Japanese were driven out of Bataan, the Philippine soldier's saw to it that Raymond was transported to an encampment of troops who had landed with Mac Arthur. Raymond, along with the surviving prisoners from the camp, were placed aboard ship and taken to a safe zone. Once they were examined, and deemed strong enough to travel, they were flown back to the United States and located in military hospitals, where they could be treated back to full recovery.

It was April, when Raymond was transported to the Wallum Lake hospital in Rhode Island and admitted to the Tuberculosis ward. The Philippine soldiers had done all they could to keep him alive, but he was still very weak and weighed just over a hundred pounds. He was still in critical condition.

That May, Ovid received a letter from the Army, informing him that Raymond had been found alive with Philippine troops, on the Isle of Bataan. It went on to say that he was moved to Wallum Lake Hospital at Pascoag Rhode Island. When Toni arrived home from work that day, Ovid only said, "A letter came from the Armed Forces department. It is about Raymond," announced Ovid.

"Where is it? What does it say? Is he--?"

No, he's alive and back here in Rhode Island. That much is good news! Ovid exclaimed. Read it yourself."

Toni was trembling, as she unfolded it and quietly absorbed the contents. "Oh Pa some Philippine soldiers found him and took care of him after he had been shot! Thank God that he is alive."

He's alive, but for how long? The combination of Tuberculosis and Malaria can kill him! Ovid responded. "Well it is too late now, but tomorrow morning we are going to drive up there and show him how happy we are that he is home and remind him how much he is loved."

The next morning after getting the children ready, and before getting on the road, Toni called her boss and told him of her situation. He empathized with her feelings, and told her to take all the time she needed.

The drive to the hospital took a little less than an hour, but the anxiety that was felt made it seem more like two. Even Ovid who rarely shows compassion, expressed his anxiety, when he said, "I didn't think Wallum Lake was so far." He was as anxious as Toni. They arrived just in time for the visiting hour. Children were not allowed in the hospital ward area so Toni told her father to go on ahead so he could have some time alone with Raymond first. "I will be there as soon as I have the children settled in the play area," she said.

When Toni entered the Tuberculosis ward, a nurse gave her a mask to wear over her nose and mouth. This alone was intimidating, but when she entered her brother's room and saw how emaciated he was it took all she had to keep from bursting into tears. She could see that even her father was shaken by what he saw. They both wondered how Raymond was able to stay alive on Bataan if he was sicker than he is now.

Raymond wept over seeing his father and sister again for the first time in over two years. He was still too week to set up, but Toni leaned over and placed her cheek to his saying, "You sure had us worried, but now everything will be all right. I am happy your back son. It will be good to get you home," said Ovid as he grasped his son's wrist tightly in his large palm.

"How is Roland? Have you heard from him?" asked Raymond. He loved and admired his older brother, and it was important for him to know that he was safe.

"Roland is fine. Pa and I received a letter from him a couple of weeks ago. His ship is somewhere in the Pacific and he has had a few exciting moments, like when a Japanese plane fired on his ship, causing some damage, and when a torpedo from a Jap submarine barely missed them. He said, other than that, he has sustained all his injuries from boxing since he joined the Navy Boxing Team. He has been very worried about you and will be glad to hear that you have made it home."

For the next three weeks, Toni and her father visited Raymond as much as possible and watched him gradually improve until they were able to bring him home. He gained most of his weight back within the following six months, and for the first time since Toni moved in with her father, a spark of happiness began a glow in the household. The children loved their giant of an uncle, who in turn loved getting their attention and giving it back.

Chapter 28

On May 7th 1945, Germany surrendered. The combined armies of the United States, Great Britain and Russia were to powerful, and had caused devastation on the German and Italian armies. Germany surrendered in April of 45.

On August 6th 1945, after President Truman was convinced that the Japanese were not about to give up unless impressed with the show of a superior force, he gave the order that the atomic bomb be dropped on Hiroshima Japan. The damage that it caused was incomprehensible and thousands of innocent citizens were killed.

On August 14th, the Japanese surrendered to the United States. A month prior to the bombing, Roland's ship had returned state side, and when President Truman announced the surrender of Japan, and the end of WWII, he and Raymond celebrated for three days. They could now get on with their lives.

Prior to his discharge from Wallum Lake, Raymond had been presented with the Purple Heart Medal, for being wounded in battle, and a few months after the war had ended he was presented with the Silver Star for gallantry in action. He remained a member of the Bataan Survivors Group until he passed away unexpectedly at age 42, while working in his yard.

Chapter 29

Life, as it was known in the little town of Sprague Ville, Rhode Island, and throughout the rest of the state, gradually got back to normal. Toni took a job closer to home at the Esmond Blanket Factory as a sewer, and was beginning to enjoy her life more since both Roland and Raymond were keeping Ovid in line.

On occasion, he would still assert his authority like the time that he chased little Dolor up the stairs and dragged him back down by one leg after his grandfather told him to take out the trash, and Dolor. seemed to ignore him. After catching Dolor, Ovid smacked him across the back of the head and bellowed "I said now, not later!"

Another time, he stabbed Ronald in the back of his hand with a fork, because he had reached across the dinner table for the butter instead of asking for it to be passed. On both occasions Toni was not home, but when she was told of the incidents by Jenny, she became very upset, and gave her father hell.

Fortunately, as time passed and the children got older, Ovid became more understanding and seemed to develop a compassionate attitude toward his grandchildren and their mother.

With her brothers home safe and Ovid nicer to live with, Toni's mind seemed more at ease and she became more approachable.

At work, she would be asked out, and on occasion she would accept a dinner date or go to a movie, but even though most of her dates were gentlemanly and she had fun, she never felt the urge to become serious and go beyond cordial feelings.

Toni had even invited her boss to dinner one evening. He was average in height and paunchy, with a relatively large nose. He had pronounced bags under his eyes and not one who the ladies would consider good looking, but he had always been a complete gentleman with Toni, and treated her like the lady she was. To Toni, he was just a good friend outside of the job, but her boss was hoping that their relationship would develop into more than that, which would never happen, especially with Dolor in the picture.

A nice dinner had been arranged with Toni, her boss, and the three children. Her brother, Raymond, still single, took his father out to eat and to a movie. The children had never met their mother's boss, but Dolor had not forgotten that his mom had mentioned the man had bags under his eyes, as she described him to Roland's new wife when Toni told her that she had invited her boss for dinner.

Toni's guest arrived shortly after six P.M., and the children where called to the living room for the introduction.

"Children, this is Mr. William McMande. He is my supervisor at the place where I work. I call him Bill, but you will always call him Mr. McMande, or sir when speaking or spoken to. Bill this is Jenny, Dolor and Ronald."

"I have looked forward to meeting you children for quite sometime. You are very lucky to have such a caring mom," Bill said.

"Yes Sir!" said Jenny and Ronald, but Dolor did not respond he only stared at the guest.

"Dolor! It is not nice to stare at someone," said Toni.

"But mom this is the man with the big bags under his eyes, you were telling Aunt Gussie about. Can I ask why he has them?"

Toni had never been so embarrassed in all of her life. With a crackle in her voice and red faced, "Dolor! You apologize to the gentleman this very minute. I have a good mind to send you to your room without dinner."

"Bu... bu... but Maa-umm?"

"You heard me young man. Tell Mr. McMande you are sorry, right now!"

Dolor sheepishly rolled his eyes in the direction of Mr. McMande as he mumbled, "I am sorry sir."

"I accept your apology Dolor. This is not the first time that someone has commented on the same thing. I guess it is hereditary, since my father also had the same problem," he responded.

"I also wish to apologize to you Bill," said Toni. It was not nice of me to have said anything to my sister-in-law."

The remainder of that evening was sensitive, and obviously somewhat false. By eight o'clock, the children were in bed sound asleep, and by 9:30, Toni and her guest had called it an evening. From that time on, Toni was very cautious about how she described her dates. She remained friends with her boss, but nothing ever developed beyond that.

For the following two to three months, she would occasionally go out with men from the town, but none of her suitors impressed her enough to create a serious relationship. Her life was mostly the children and her employment.

The thought of getting married again, rarely entered her mind. After all, not only was she working full time, raising a family, and trying to keep her father happy, but she also had her hands full with Dolor., now ten years old and very mischievous.

Teasing his sister and brother came in the package and could be tolerated within reason, but taking his grandfathers cigarettes, to smoke behind the outhouse, and setting fire to the dry field in back, was another story.

Chapter 30

1946 was an exciting year for Toni and Dolor. That summer, the fire dept. had to be called out twice. The back field had caught fire when Dolor was smoking behind the out house, and a second time when he tried to make smoke signals from the burning trash that Ovid had set on fire in their metal trash barrel.

Toni feared that Dolor would not only cause greater property damage, but that he would catch himself on fire. She tried impressing him of the danger by lecturing him, but that did not work. She restricted him, and that didn't work. Ultimately, she resorted to spanking him with a belt, but nothing worked until one day he was caught lighting matches very close to the kerosene by the back entry.

It was on a Saturday afternoon when everyone was home doing their thing. The children were all supposed to be out playing in the back yard. As Toni went to check on them, out of the corner of her eye, she observed a movement behind the kerosene barrel. It was Dolor he was lighting matches that he had taken from his grandfather's cigarette table.

"Oh! My God Dolor! What are you thinking? Give me them match's this instant, and go into the house!" yelled Toni, as she followed her son, trembling and thinking about what could have happened.

The advice she had been given by Roland, which was to let him feel the heat of a match on the tip of two or three fingers, if he ever played with fire again, also came to her mind. It was advice that she thought she could never act upon and hoped it would not ever have to be considered.

In the kitchen, Toni looked at Dolor and tried to explain what a dangerous thing he had done. "Do you realize that you could have been burned to death, or burned down our home had the kerosene in that barrel ignited? What is it going to take to get you to stop playing with fire?

"I won't do it again Mommy." Dolor responded.

"That is what you have told me each time, you were caught, and here we are again. No, Dolor! I love you to much, and I would feel that I was a bad mother if I did not do all I could to stop you from this dangerous thing you are doing."

With tears in her eyes she held Dolor close by her and lit a match. She then held two of his finger tips over the flame for a moment, saying, "This is only your fingers. Think about how much it would hurt if your whole body was on fire." She then placed his fingers in ice, and they cried together.

"Mommy feels very bad when she has to punish her children, but when I do, I want you to remember that it is done because I love you and I am trying to guide you to becoming good adults, one day."

From that time on Dolor never played with fire, but to know him was to know that a potential disaster was in the making, like the time he was asked to take care of his Uncle Raymond's prize Rhode Island Red, chickens. Toni, in turmoil over the disciplinary action that she had taken with Dolor needed someone to talk with, so she turned to her brother Raymond. It was then that they came up with the idea of giving him things to do that would teach him more responsibility.

Raymond was leaving town on business, and while he was gone, his prize chickens would need feeding and watering. The temperature had been holding between ninety and one hundred degrees with ninety percent humidity all week. The only way to get cool was by the garden hose, or going swimming, during the day, and sleeping outside at night. The responsibility of caring for the chickens seemed like a perfect chore to give Dolor, so his uncle took him aside and explained how important it was to feed, water and let the chickens out of the coup everyday.

"Do a good job, and I will pay you $5.00." Dolor's uncle told him.

"Wow! $5.00 I will do a good job uncle," he responded excitedly.

"Now remember, be sure they have plenty of water, and the coop is open during the day, so they can get out in the fresh air. If you don't open their door and side window, it will get so hot in there, and they could suffocate. After dinner I want you to be sure and chase them back inside, and close up the coop so a fox doesn't get in and eat them. Do you think that you can do all that, with out a problem?" asked his uncle.

"Yes uncle! I can do it," Dolor said with enthusiasm.

That Saturday, Dolor got up and took care of his responsibility before breakfast, and by six thirty that evening, he saw to it that the chickens were back in their coop and it was closed up tight.

Sunday was something different. Dolor was allowed to stay up and listen to the radio with Jenny until 9:00 P.M. the night before, so he did not wake up until his mom called out, "Common children it is time to get up and dress for church." Within less than an hour, the family was dressed and off to Sunday Mass at St. Phillips Catholic church.

Ovid did not go to church, and departed shortly after, in his 1929 Model A Ford, and drove to his sister's house for the day. The chickens remained in the coop. Toni and the children got home shortly before 10:00 A.M. By then, the temperature had reached, at least seventy-five, and it was climbing.

As they walked from the car to the house, Toni said, "It is going to be a very hot day, so I would like the three of you to change into cool play cloths, while I fix something to eat." Later today, we will go swimming at Mountain Dale pond and try to keep cool. This of course, excited the children, and completely eliminated the possibility that Ray might recall his obligation to the chickens.

It was about 12:45, and the three children were playing under the giant maple shade tree in the front yard, when Toni called them.

"Common children, it is time to get into your swim suits, so we can go to Mountain Dale." In a very short time, they were excitedly on their way.

The temperature had climbed close to ninety degrees in the sun, with seventy percent humidity. The coop had to be at least one hundred and twenty on the inside. If the chickens hadn't suffocated, they soon would.

Everyone was gone, and Toni's brother Raymond, was not due to arrive home for at least two more hours. Everyone was having a good time swimming. The children played with neighborhood friends, and Toni enjoyed setting in the sun watching them and chatting with the parents around her. It was one of those days when time was not important. Or was it?

"Let's go children. It is almost four thirty, and I have to prepare dinner when we get home," Toni said, as she called Jenny, Dolor, and Ronnie out of the water.

At home, Toni parked her car in the usual place at the back of the house, and was surprised to see her brother, Raymond sitting on the steps. "Are you waiting for us she asked, with a smile as they got out?"

"Oh yes!" He responded with a sober look. I want Dolor to look over at the chicken house and tell me what he sees."

It took only a moment for Dolor to realize what his uncle was talking about, and with the look of embarrassment, he said "Oh no! I forgot the chickens. I will go let them out right now."

"You are too late! They are all dead from suffocating in the intense heat because you failed in your responsibility to open the coop."

Dolor tried to hold back his tears, but was unable, as he ran into the house sobbing.

The next morning, Dolor's uncle asked him to assist in the burial of the fifteen prize Rhode Island Red hens. He humbly agreed, and worked hard assisting his uncle, hoping for a sign of forgiveness.

His uncle, well aware of how precious life is to man and animal, remained resolute, but showed compassion as he said, "From now on, I hope that when ever you agree to be responsible in a situation where a life or lives could be affected, whether human or otherwise, you will recall what happened here,"

"I will uncle, I will. I am very sorry for what I did."

"I believe you are! Now let's put it behind us and go have something to eat. What do you think about a chicken salad sandwich?" His uncle said, as he laughed and patted Dolor on the head. The subject of the prized chicken's, was never brought up again.

Chapter 31

Dolor continued with an occasional prank, but they were generally well thought out. Like on a foggy Halloween night when the fog was so thick that a driver had to keep his eye on the white center line or possibly travel off of the road and have an accident. That evening, Jenny, Dolor, and Ronnie, and three boys from the neighborhood, had been out trick-or-treating, but had only visited a few houses because it was so hard to see through the fog.

While they were out, Dolor and the oldest of the other three boys had noticed how slow cars were moving and how important the white center line was to the drivers. This gave them an idea for a Halloween trick.

After walking Jenny home at about eight o'clock, the boys obtained permission to stay out for one more hour. The five of them immediately went to the barn where Ovid kept his paint, and removed a gallon of black and a gallon of white. They then walked approximately one hundred yards beyond their houses where the narrow two lane road begins a gradual curve to the left, and continues a short distance before coming to a bridge that crosses a shallow river.

At the beginning of the curve, Dolor and his friends began painting the center line black, occasionally running to hide in the weeds at the edge of the road when a car would pass by. They painted out the line all the way to within fifty feet of the bridge, where they changed to white and painted a misleading line that lead to the shallow river. There were very few cars on the road because of the pea soup fog. Those that were out had to move slowly and use the white center line for a beacon.

After completing their artistic undertaking, the boys returned the paint to the barn, cleaned the brushes in turpentine, and placed everything in order.

For the following half-hour or so, they sat on the front steps of Ovid's house and waited for a car to pass. When one finally did, they sat quietly waiting to hear a noise that would indicate it had gone off of the road, but all remained quiet. Having heard nothing by nine thirty, the boys agreed to call it a night and they went home home.

The following morning, everyone was up early. Toni was in the kitchen preparing breakfast, Ovid was out in his work shop, and the children were in the living room, quietly waiting to hear their mom call out, "Come and eat, while it is hot."

Then there came a knock on the front door. "One of you children see who that is, please!" asked Toni.

At that moment, Dolor jumped from his chair and ran to the door. In the opened door, there stood a tall man in a dark blue uniform, wearing a beige Stetson, and knee high brown boots. On his right hip he wore a holstered pistol, and on his chest there glistened a gold badge. He was from the impressive and intimidating Rhode Island State Police. "Good morning son. Is your mother or father at home?" he asked.

Dolor stood in awe as he looked at this giant of a man, who all boys his age were impressed with whenever one would be seen in the neighborhood. Now one was standing at his front door. What could he want? Dolor thought to himself.

"Who is there Dolor?" Toni called out.

"It's a trooper, mom."

"A what?" responded Toni, as she walked to the front door. Oh! Hello officer! Please come in. I am Antoinette Emond, how may I help you?"

"I am sorry to be bothering you on a Saturday morning like

this, ma'am, but an incident took place a short distance from here, which could have caused a fellow officer to be injured, and I am investigating the matter."

"Jenny, please take Dolor and Ronnie to the kitchen, and dish out their breakfast for mother. Then go call your grandfather."

"Well, I don't know if I will be of any help officer, but please sit down and make your self comfortable. Would you like a cup of coffee?"

"Yes Ma'am! That would taste good about now. Thank you!"

Within a few minutes, Ovid came into the living room, and was introduced to the officer by Toni, before she went for the coffee. "What is this all about?" Ovid asked.

"It is about what appears to be an intended Halloween prank, by some youngsters, that has backfired into something more serious. I will explain everything when Mrs. Emond returns from the kitchen."

Toni soon returned with the coffee, and a homemade cinnamon role. "You have excited my curiosity officer, so will you please tell us what this is all about," Toni said as she sat across from her guest.

"Last evening, Halloween evening, to be exact, it was extremely foggy. I assume that you both drive?" the trooper queried.

"Yes we do." Ovid responded.

"Then you know how dangerous it is to drive in a dense or pea soup fog, and how important the white center line is at that time. Anyway, some youngsters (I assume they were youngsters), took it upon themselves to play a prank and paint the center line black up to the river-bridge, where they changed it to a white line leading off of the road. This would cause an unsuspecting driver to end up in the river.

Fortunately, a fellow officer who travels this road frequently, caught on, and put out flares after almost becoming the first victim!"

"So why have you come to us?" Toni interrupted. Do you think that my boys had something to do with it?"

"Right now Ma'am, I have no real suspects, but some of your neighbors did see your two boys and the Donahue boys, out in that general area on Halloween night, so I would like to ask them a few questions, if you don't mind?"

"No I don't mind. I would hope that they would never do something like what you have described, but let's talk to them. Boys come in to the living room the officer would like to speak to you," Toni called out.

Dolor and Ronnie had finished their breakfast, and were helping Jenny clean up when they heard their mom call. They had no idea what it was all about, but were excited to find out, and ran to the living room. "Yes Mom!" said Dolor, as he sat down by her gazing at the Trooper as if he idolized him.

Ronnie sat on the floor in front of his grandfather also gazing up at this big man in a dark uniform, while in his own mind, comparing the officer to a picture of Hitler's police, which his uncle had shown him.

"Dolor, were you and Ronnie out with the Donahue boys on Halloween night?" the officer asked.

"Yes sir! We went trick or treating."

"Did you happen to play any tricks, like painting the white line black?" the officer asked.

By now, Toni's heart was pounding as she nervously waited for an answer. She was aware that even her boys were capable of pulling an occasional prank, or performing an experiment to find out what could happen, but it was to much to believe that they would go so far as to cause a car to go into the river.

Dolor looked at his grandfather, knowing what to expect, when he would hear that it was his paint they had used, and then toward his mother, thinking of how he had broken her heart with his prior escapades. He thought that if he said no, and they later found out he lied he would only delay the inevitable, and his punishment would be more severe. "Yes we did, sir!" Dolor answered as he looked in the direction of his little brother, who knew then that they were in big trouble.

Ronnie had a good idea of what his mom was going to do, but his greatest fear was what this Trooper would do to them. His imagination was running wild. He could picture himself being tortured to death, like in the stories he had been told by his uncles, of Hitler's police tactics.

"Did you have any idea when you performed this prank, of how dangerous it was, and that you could have caused someone to be seriously injured?" asked the Trooper.

"No sir, we just thought it would be funny if a car ended up in the creek. We didn't think that someone might get hurt. I really am sorry!"

"M...m...m... meee tt-to!" said Ronnie, in a low quivering voice.

"Were the Donahue boys with you?" asked Toni

"Yes." said Dolor.

"What now?" Toni asked the State Trooper.

"Well! I will go and have a talk with the Donahue's, and then present my findings to the chief for a final decision. I doubt that there will be any repercussions since nothing but a gallon or two of paint, and a little labor is the only cost to the state, but I want you boys to remember, that you were very lucky to get off so easy."

"Yes Sir! We won't ever do anything like that again sir. Thank you sir!" the boys said loud and clear, taking deep breaths.

"Thank you officer! said Toni. The state may forgive them, but the boys know that I also have rules, and that there are consequences for violating those rules. They won't be playing with the Donahue boys or anyone else for at least two weeks, and I will see that they are so busy that they won't have time to get into trouble."

"Yes Ma'am!" responded the Trooper, smiling and shaking the hands of Toni and Ovid, as he departed.

"I hope you two have learned a lesson from this. In my day, I would have been horse whipped by my father, for a wrong half as serious," said Ovid, as he walked out and went to his workshop.

"Well boys, what do you have to say for yourselves? Haven't I been a good mother? I have tried to give you a good home with the things that many other children would appreciate, and don't have. You know right from wrong, and still, you do things that upset me. I understand wanting to have fun and even getting into trouble for something minor, but this was serious. I am very unhappy about this." Toni lectured the boys, hoping to reach their compassionate side, which she did.

Soon, both boys went to her and gave her a hug, as they expressed their sorrow for hurting her. "We know how wrong we were mom, and we are now ready to take our punishment," said Dolor, with Ronnie standing by his side, wishing his big brother would shut up.

For the next two weeks, the boys did not get to play with their friends, and were kept very busy doing chores for their mom and Ovid, and even the dishes for their sister. They had learned their lesson, and would at least think over the consequences of the next prank or experiment, they tried out.

Chapter 32

Life in the Emond household continued to go as well as could be expected. The boys continued their pranks, with better judgment, except for the time a neighborhood bully had pressed his luck one to many times. He was Skeeter Randall, the typical square headed, no necked, no brains, blonde haired, green eyed jerk, who made his father proud, by beating up kids smaller than him.

Skeeter often showed up unexpectedly, and would waist no time trying to pick a fight. He was big for his age, but slow on his feet, which Dolor had figured out, so a plan to out smart him, and hopefully keep him from returning, was put into affect.

Dolor would get Skeeter to chase him around the perimeter of the garden, and along side of the barn, where he and Ronnie had removed some of the boards covering the sewage that came from the barn toilet. They used straw to camouflage the open area, and Ray new just when to jump. The plan worked perfectly.

Only two days after developing their race course, Skeeter ate some crap. A fare and just consequence for all the crap he had given the smaller kids in the neighborhood.

It wasn't long after that, Skeeter and his father moved away, probably because the boy's uncle Ray had a meaningful talk with Mr. Randall when they crossed paths in town; a few days after his son got his dues.

The story of their encounter went something like this... Skeeter's father saw the boy's uncle walking by the hardware store, and rudely approached him. "You're the uncle of those boy's who live in T.K. Windsor's old house aren't you?"

"Yes I am!" "I don't believe I have ever met you."

"I happen to be the father of the boy your nephews pushed into the outhouse shit the other day, so you had better take warning that we Randall's don't tolerate anybody messing with our young-ins."

"Well first of all Mr. Randall, it sounds to me like you are making a threat against two little boys. I don't think that will set well with the police, who I understand do not have a whole lot of respect for you and yours. Secondly, my nephews have told me about your son and his antics, bullying them and other kids in the neighborhood, so it only seems just that he met up with consequences befitting his kind. Finally, if you know what is good for you, and you want to remain healthy, you will stay a long way from me and my family. I am a busy man Mr. Randall, so please get out of my way."

"You don't scare me!" Randall said, as he backed out of Ray's way. He was never heard from after that encounter.

Neither the boy's nor their uncle ever told Toni the story of Skeeter's encounter with the out-house cesspool.

It was 1947, and the boys were staying out of trouble. Jenny had met some girl friends from the church and had been spending a lot of time at church activities. By the time she turned fourteen Jenny had developed such a strong belief in the Virgin Mary that she would get up early, five days a week, during her Summer vacation and walk three miles to church, where the rosary would be prayed.

She was a daughter that would make any mother very proud. In the mean time, Toni was able to relax more and think about her future. She had never intended to live with her father so long and was developing a strong drive to get out on her own.

She had been thinking and wondering about Whitey more than ever. She wondered if he was still alive and what was he doing? She still saw her aunt Addie quite often, and had confided in her about her feelings towards Whitey.

Chapter 33

Whitey was back in town, and looking very dapper. He had retired from the Merchant Marines and was researching the possibility of venturing into his own textile business. He'd only been back a little more then a month, so his presence in the small New England town of Greenville hadn't reached Sprague Ville, were Toni was residing.

Whitey had also seen some action during the war, and was fortunate that none of the merchant ships he had been on were struck by enemy torpedoes even though there were some very near misses. There was also the time that he partied all night in New York city, and his ship left without him because he over slept.

Two days later that ship was torpedoed and sunk leaving no survivors. The recipe for Whitey's life was a mixture of luck and the drive to see what was over the next hill. He had already seen more of the world, and adventured beyond most men's expectations. Had he been born a century sooner he probably would have been a famous explorer.

Addie, who also lived in Greenville, had met Whitey only once, prior to Toni and him splitting up, so it was unlikely that she would recognize him even if they bumped into each other.

But as fate would have it, a few days after Toni had told her aunt that she was thinking about Whitey, they did bump into each other.

Addie was rushing out of the post office, and he accidentally brushed her on his way in, knocking a piece of mail from her hand.

"I am sorry Ma'am." said Whitey, as he picked up the envelope and handed it to her.

"It's my fault," responded Addie, as she looked directly at him. Why do I have a feeling that I know you from somewhere? Are you from Greenville?"

"Yes ma'am and isn't your name Addie? Isn't Antoinette Paulhus your niece?'

"Yes to both questions, but I still don't know your name."

"Forgive me, my name is Fred White, but I am known to most people as Whitey. I had the pleasure of meeting you one time about seventeen years ago, when I was very much in love with your niece. How is she doing?"

"Oh, she is doing just fine now, but she really had it tough for a while after the loss of her husband. It has only been in the past two years, that her life has settled down. She has a lot of fortitude and character."

"I had heard that she was married, and had three children, but that was just before the war had broken out. I never heard anymore after that. I am sorry to hear that she is a widow."

"She has been a widow for almost ten years now, and I would say she is ready to meet another good man," said Addie with a girlish grin. "Coincidentally, if I recall correctly, it was just a short time ago, that Toni brought your name up. I think she said she had been wondering if you were still at sea, and if you were married."

"When you see her, please tell her no to both questions, and I would really enjoy a chance to see her again," responded Whitey.

"I have a better idea. Next Friday evening I am having a small gathering at my house and I am sure that Toni will be there. We play cards, tell jokes, and sing a little. Why don't you come and join us?"

"I would enjoy that very much, that is if you are sure I wouldn't be imposing on the others."

"I am sure! After all, it is my party, and my house, and the guests know better than to complain about whom I invite. Anyway, I will expect you to help liven it up if it starts to get dull. I won't tell Toni that you will be there so you can surprise her."

"Ok, I'll be there." "You can count on it!" Whitey exclaimed.

That evening Adie called Toni to confirm that she would be attending the gathering at her place. "Don't forget, I am expecting you at my place this Friday."

"I haven't forgotten, aunt Adie, but I am not sure if I will make it. After all, I really don't know any of the people who you have invited!"

"Oh, I wouldn't be so sure! There is one guest who I have invited especially for you, and I know that you have met him before."

"Who is he?" Toni asked.

"If I told you that it wouldn't be a surprise. Anyway, I promised my guest that I would keep it a secret."

"I can't imagine who this secret guest could be, but now that you have excited my curiosity, you can count on me being there."

"Great! I will be expecting you around seven so you can assist me in the preparations before the guests begin arriving at eight.

For the remainder of the week, Toni was like a teenager looking forward to her first date. She could not stop wondering about the man who according to her aunt she would know when she was reintroduced to him at the party.

When the time came, Toni arrived at her aunt's house early and assisted in the preparations. She was dressed elegantly, yet refined. There was no doubt that Whitey would be very pleased. "Our guests will be arriving soon and I would appreciate it if you would be at my side so that I may introduce them to my beautiful niece," said Addie. Her anxiousness to surprise her niece was as great as Toni's was to meet this mystery person.

Soon the guests began arriving, many of them coupled up and considerably older than Toni, but she remained anxious to meet the one who would possibly bring back memories for her and excitement to the party.

By nine o'clock all the guests except Whitey had arrived and both Addie and Toni became concerned that he was not going to show. "I'm sorry honey! I can't imagine why my special guest hasn't arrived. He promised that he would be here to surprise you!" Addie exclaimed, while she and Toni were in the kitchen preparing more finger food.

"It's alright, Aunt Addie! Maybe something unexpected came up, and he has been detained. Why don't you go and play cards with your guests while I finish up here!

"All right, but I expect you to join us, as soon as you are done."

No sooner had Addie sat down to one of the four card tables in the living room, the doorbell rang. It was Whitey. "I apologize" he said, as he shook Addie's hand. Two of my old ship mates showed up unexpectedly and I had to talk my way out the door."

"Come in, come in!" Once the introductions to her guests had been completed, Addie took Whitey's hand and said, "Toni is feeling a little out of place so she is in the kitchen pretending to be busy." Entering the kitchen, with Whitey still in hand, "Aren't you finished yet?" Addie asked.

Standing with her back to Adie and Whitey, "Almost. I will be out in a minute." Toni responded.

To that, Addie quickly came back with, "I have brought someone to assist you so you can join in the fun sooner."

Toni turned to meet her helper, and in an expression of disbelief, smiling delightfully "Fred? This is a surprise. I never thought that I would see you again."

"Well, do I get a hug? Whitey asked. After all, it has been at least seventeen or eighteen years, since we last spoke!"

"Of course you do," said Toni, as she walked to him with her arms outstretched. I just can't believe it."

"I'll get back to my guests, and leave you two alone." said Addie, leaving the kitchen with a smile.

"Thanks for such a nice surprise. We will be out in a few minutes." Toni responded.

Like a couple of young lovers, Whitey and Toni held hands as they sat at the kitchen table and talked about all that had taken place since they last saw each other. "I was sorry to hear that your husband had passed on! He was so young! It must have been real hard for you, raising three children on your own, especially during the war years."

"I admit there were times that I wondered if I would make it, but here I am. I thank God and the blessed Virgin for giving me the strength to continue on with my life."

"So do I. I mean that I thank God for not only keeping you strong, but also for letting me find you again. Would it be possible for me to call on you next week, after I conclude some business?"

"I would like that," answered Toni. I am curious, haven't you ever married?"

"No, I never did! My life just didn't seem to allow for that kind of a commitment once I began studying for advancement and taking classes on the textile industry. Besides, I have spent the past twenty years out on the ocean or in a foreign land, and have returned to the East coast only four times to visit family. It turned out for the best after you refused my proposal about eighteen years ago. I can see that now, so would it be alright if I stop by next Wednesday, around seven? Whitey quickly asked like a teenager with a crush.

"I will look forward to seeing you again!" said Toni.

Before they realized it the time had passed quickly, and the guests were leaving. Toni had taken the finger food in to them earlier, but after that she and Whitey remained in the kitchen, where they could be aloof from the activity in the living-room. Addie did not mind because she was excited for them, and understood the situation.

From that night on, Toni and Whitey continued to see each other quite often. During the week Whitey would come to the house at least once or twice, just to set and talk with Toni and her father. On the weekend he would take Toni to a dinner and dancing.

Toni's dad liked Whitey because he was well traveled, and also, because he always brought a quart of beer which they would share while sitting in the living room discussing various topics. Whitey would vividly describe how the people in countries that the average American had only heard about in school were ruled, and kept depressed by ruthless leaders. He emphasized that a democracy was by far, better than a dictatorship, but also believed that in America, the U.S. government was actually run by the wealthiest men in the world, and therefore all major decisions affecting the economy, would favor the rich. He said that the little people needed to stick together, or the giant U.S. government would eventually rule them like the dictatorship they tried to leave behind when they departed from their European home land

Whitey was well read. His geographical knowledge was parallel to that of one who majored in that subject. He had also become very knowledgeable in textiles, which he had become schooled in while a merchant marine in the oil shipping market. Whitey's study of textiles, an oil commodity, was based on a dream that one day, by this knowledge and his drive for success he would become an entrepreneur in the manufacturing of cloth material and reap the financial benefit. Since his return to New England, he had been involved in establishing such a business and was already in production before finding Toni again.

The loving couple continued seeing each other as often as possible, till the time had come for Whitey to pop the big question. His business was doing well and he felt that he could now give the lady he loved, and her children, the life he thought they deserved.

It was on one of those beautiful New England evenings in June, when the temperature was in the seventies, and the aroma of wild flowers filled the air, that Whitey chose to ask Toni if she would marry him. They had just finished a fine dinner at Tom's Lodge, located in the country on the north end of the state and were sipping an after dinner liquor when Whitey reached into the pocket of his suit coat and pulled out a small box.

During dinner, he and Toni had been discussing their destiny, and the things they would like to see come true in the near future, so the time seemed right to pop the question. As Whitey opened the box to an exquisite half-karat diamond ring, he nervously said.

"The first time I asked for your hand in marriage, you were wise enough to say no because we were both too young. Since that time I have often wondered if I would ever get a second chance, and as fate would have it, I believe it is now. Will you marry me?"

With tears in her eyes and a smile that projected the pinnacle of happiness, Toni said, "Yes! I will be proud to be your wife." She removed the ring from the box and placed it on her finger.

With that, Whitey excitedly said, "I would like to wait until we can find some land and have a house built. I think we can do that and still get married next spring. That way I can move you and the children into a nice new home shortly after we become man and wife. Would that be alright with you?"

"That would be wonderful, but wouldn't that be a lot to take on all at once, financially?" Toni responded.

"I don't think so. My business has been doing well and it is still growing. We just got a new contract with Botany 500, and it looks like we could be getting one or two government contracts, also. Let's go for it!"

"Do you have an idea of where to look for land?" Toni asked.

"It just so happens, I do. A few months ago when I new that I would be asking you to marry me, I met with a contractor about building the house."

"I asked about available land and he told me of an old retired, school teacher widow who wants to sell off some land which she no longer has any use for. It is located about five miles north of here and easily accessible. She wants one hundred dollars an acre, and I figure that we can afford at least twenty two acres. The contractor, who has a good reputation, will be happy to assist us in designing our house, once we have the land to put it on."

"You really have been busy, haven't you? It sure sounds exciting to me. I can't wait to get started!" Toni responded.

"What do you think about going to see the lady who owns the land next Saturday?"

"I think that is a great idea."

"Good! We will take the children along for the ride, and go for some ice-cream afterwards."

The following Saturday, a contract to purchase twenty-two acres of partially cleared forestland, was consummated. A week later, Whitey and Toni met with the contractor and rough plans for their dream house were drawn up.

Within one month after the land purchase, the plans were finalized and construction was underway. After the removal of several trees, a bulldozer was brought in and the hole for a large basement was dug. The foundation was poured, and a week later, the construction of the house began.

The carpenters worked six days a week, so that the electrician, plumber, dry wall-man, tile layer, and painter could get in and have the house ready to be moved into by the middle of October.

Chapter 34

Toni was excited about the opportunity to decorate a new home once again. She had some furnishings she brought with her to her father's house, but nowhere near enough for a two story, twenty five hundred square foot home. The thought of purchasing new furnishings was exciting, but not as exciting as the thought that she will be getting married in a week.

They had a small wedding, at St. Phillips church with only a few family members and friends attending, and than went off on a one week honeymoon to Niagara Falls, upstate New York. The children stayed with their grandfather, which seemed like an eternity to them, but all in all everything went well, and soon their mom was back home with their new dad.

Jenny and Dolor remained aloof of Whitey, but Ronald, in need of more male bonding than his grandfather had to offer, sought attention by going to Whitey. "Oh boy, I have a dad."

He said as he sat with Whitey, only to receive the unexpected, "Not now, your mother and I just got home and we are tired."

This hurt Toni, because she knew how much her son needed and wanted a father. She did not anticipate what had happened, but put it out of her mind by telling herself her husband was tired from the long trip.

Plans had been made to move into the new house on the

upcoming weekend. Whitey recruited the help of his brother-in-law Ted, and borrowed his fully enclosed trailer. That weekend, the men loaded the trailer while Toni and the children packed the car, leaving only enough room for her and Jenny. Dolor asked to ride in the trailer, and Ron would ride with his Uncle Ted, who followed in his car. Whitey also chose to ride inside of the trailer to hold a large antique mirror from falling.

"Fred, I don't think that it is a good idea for you and Dolor to ride in the trailer. What if it disconnected from the car and turned over or hit another car, you could both be killed!" Toni exclaimed.

"You worry too much. Let's go and get this move over with, so we can stay in the new house tonight," Whitey responded.

The hitch on the trailer was not compatible with the ball connection on the car, and a good jolt, could cause it to disconnect. Also, there were no safety chains to keep the trailer attached to the car if the hitch did let go.

Both Toni and Ted tried to talk Fred into waiting until they could borrow a truck, but he wouldn't hear of it. That afternoon they began their trek to their new home in the country eight miles away and mostly up hill.

The country roads were very narrow, and forty miles per hour seemed fast, so Toni made it a point to maintain a speed between thirty and thirty-five. Each time they hit a bump or a dip in the road she held her breath in fear that the trailer would disconnect.

When they got to within two or three miles from their destination, they turned onto a main highway with two lanes each way. This was the road that most travelers from Rhode Island and Connecticut took to Boston. Toni felt somewhat relieved when they got onto this open highway which was maintained significantly better than most, so she increased her speed to forty-five miles per hour.

The next mile or so was a gradual uphill grade and there was no concern for a bump that may cause the trailer to disconnect, Toni thought. She had completely forgotten about a dip where the road met with the end of a bridge, which quite often caused passengers to bump their heads on the inside roof when driven over at a speed of forty or more.

From one end of the bridge to the other was about one hundred yards, and the east end, having a smooth approach, gave no clue to a driver that they needed to slow down. From the time they drove onto the bridge until they reached the other side, only took about thirty seconds, and all hell broke loose.

Within seconds, the front of the car entered the dip at the west end of the bridge, and then the back end dropped in causing the trailer to completely disconnect from the car and begin rolling backward with Whitey and Dolor locked inside.

Ted, who was following, immediately swerved right to avoid the trailer, and stopped on the shoulder. Toni also pulled to a stop, got out, and ran back to Ted. "Oh God, it's not stopping, it's going to go over the cliff." said Toni.

The bridge extended across a one hundred foot deep ravine to a river below. If the trailer did not stop, Whitey nor Dolor could possibly survive such a fall. If the impact did not kill them, they would be crushed by the contents.

The trailer had tilted to the rear, and the frame was hitting the surface of the road as it rolled backward. With luck it would slow and get hung up on something as it crossed the paved shoulder, and onto the ten or twelve feet of rough ground, before reaching the edge of the cliff.

"Look! Look! It is going to the right. If it continues rolling backward, the corner could strike that big rock and send it away from the edge." said Ted.

"Oh God don't take my son and husband away from me. Please stop the trailer safely." Toni thought to herself as she watched.

No sooner had she completed her silent prayer, the right corner of the trailer struck the large rock, causing the trailer to spin and come to stop within less than ten feet from the edge. Ted was the first to get to the rear door and open it up. Both Whitey and Dolor were pinned against the wall, by a dresser and mirror they had been trying to control. Miraculously neither were injured, nor were any bones broken.

"What the hell happened?" Whitey asked.

"Exactly what I was afraid would happen. The hitch let go when I hit that dip." Toni responded as she pointed in the direction of the west end of the bridge. You are lucky that you both weren't killed.

Suppose a car or a truck was passing when the trailer was careening across the road? I am still trembling from the thought of what could have happened."

"Well, it's all over now, and no one was injured. Look, Dolor is even smiling. It's the most exciting experience he has ever had," Whitey responded.

It was as if the incident was a part of daily life for Whitey. It was hard to tell if he feared much if anything, because of his nonchalant mannerisms. "It doesn't look like the trailer is any worse for ware, so let's see if we can get it hooked up and finish our adventure."

"I'm still shaking, so you had better drive Fred," Responded Toni.

"Ok I'll drive! Dolor, do you want to ride in the trailer, or with your uncle?" asked Fred, with a grin on his face, knowing what his answer would be.

"I'll go with Uncle Ted."

From that point they drove slowly to their destination, and still got moved in before dark. The cold weather was on the way and there was still a lot to do both inside and out. So while Jenny and her mom dealt with the interior, Whitey and the boys tackled the task of getting at least two cords of wood cut and stacked for the winter. On weekdays, Whitey had to tend to his textile business, and the boys were left with the job of sawing up the fallen trees. This was very hard work for them, but between their moans and groans they got the job done.

The living room had a large fireplace which would help keep down the usage of heating oil during the cold weather.

Warm evenings in front of the fireplace were greatly appreciated, and the boys knew then that their hard work was all worth it.

The acreage of land that they had purchased had been sectioned off with stone walls, at least seventy five years prior, when a farmer had owned the land. Most of the land was heavily overgrown with trees and underbrush. There had been enough land cleared to build the house and to have a large front lawn, but it was Tony and Fred's plan to clear even more, to make room for a large back yard, a gazebo, and a large garden.

Chapter 35

In the next four years the business grew rapidly, and all of the planned projects around their home were completed. Whitey and Toni, who was more often called Antoinette Emily, or just Emily, were often referred to as that well to do family out in the country.

Whenever they were in church or in town shopping, they would always be well dressed, and traveled in a fine new Mercury automobile. On Sunday after church, Fred would take the family for a ride to someplace they had never seen before. They would have dinner in a nice restaurant, and then stop for ice cream, on the way home. The children got a taste of the life that they had only heard about before their mom married Whitey.

They were more fortunate than most, because they had experienced the difficulties of only getting by financially, vs. living the upper middle class life. Their friends were treated as equals, no matter how poor or well off they were. Jenny was able to go to an all girls Catholic academy, and the boys went to the best all boys Catholic academy, in the state. Life was good for Toni and her children, but that was about to change.

Chapter 36

Whitey's business had progressed so well, that he purchased a larger factory and more equipment. He employed between ninety and one hundred employees in the factory and had to increase his book keeping staff in the office, so he hired an accountant who was known to most, as Casey. He was placed in charge of the clerical and book keeping department, and was given the sole responsibility of all outgoing and incoming monies, which was against good business ethics.

Toni did not agree that one person should have the financial control of a company, but when she expressed that to Whitey, he responded "You worry too much. Stick to the kitchen, and let me run the business."

The business continued to grow, as more orders for cloth came in. Whitey was able to hire several family members who needed the work, so to them, and those who knew him, he was a God send for the small town of Pascoag, Rhode Island, until one day in 1953.

That morning, Whitey arrived at the factory to find everyone standing outside, and the police guarding pad locked doors. As he got out of his vehicle and walked toward the factory doors, he was approached by two men in dark suits who identified themselves as IRS agents. "What the hell is going on here?" He asked.

"It's like this, Mr. White. The Internal Revenue Service is shutting you down, for tax evasion."

"What? Where the hell is Casey? Has anyone seen Casey?"

"Have you IRS people spoken to the book keeper? There has to be a mistake!"

"No Mr. White, this is not a mistake, and no we haven't spoken to your book keeper. We have been waiting to speak with you, before speaking with anyone else."

"What about my employees, can't they go inside and work? Are you going to stop them from making a living?"

"We have our orders Mr. White, and those orders are to lock up your factory until further notice, and no one is allowed inside. You may as well tell your employees to go home."

"Who in the hell do you people think you are? Why wasn't I notified about this so-called nonpayment of taxes? How can you just walk in here like this, and lock me out, with out giving me some kind of notice?"

"The IRS has sent you several inquiries beginning three years ago, and there has never been a response to any of those letters."

"The last letter was sent to you ninety days ago, warning you of an impending legal action, which was also ignored. That is why we are here, Mr. White."

"I don't get it! My book keeper opens all the business mail. You mean to tell me, he was receiving letters from the IRS, and throwing them away? Just a moment, let me ask my secretary if she recalls seeing any letters? She is still standing over there. Mary! Please come over here, I want to ask you a question."

"Yes! What is it Mr. White?"

"Mary, do you recall ever seeing any mail come across your desk with an Internal Revenue return address?"

"Oh yes! Mr. White. I saw several, but after the first one Mr. Casey instructed me to give them to him unopened."

"That son of a b..... Casey. He is behind all of this!" Whitey exclaimed.

"Thank you Mary! We aren't going to open the factory today! Will you please tell the others they can go home, and that I will be in touch once this matter is resolved."

"He knew that you would be here today, and that is why he hasn't shown," responded Mary as she walked away.

"I don't know what the problem is, Mr. White, but I suggest that you sit down with your attorney right away and see if you can come up with a good defense," the IRS agent suggested.

"We will be taking your books with us for a thorough audit, so I recommend that you have your attorney give us a call in a week or so. We will also be leaving a security guard to watch the place so it would not be a good idea for anyone to try and get in. Good luck Mr. White!"

Whitey's face was red, and his eyes were swelled up, like he could cry at any moment as he watched the men from the Internal Revenue Service, drive away. "How could this be?" He asked his brother Harold, who had come over to be with him once the agents had walked away. Do you think that Casey has been keeping the money that was supposed to be paid to the IRS?"

"I don't know Fred responded Harold, but I will do all that I can to help get you out of this predicament. Let's go see If Casey is at home, and have a talk with him.

Whitey and his brother Harold drove to Casey's house, about twenty minutes away. When they arrived, they found only Casey's wife at home, and she claimed that she did not know where he was. She said that he had left the same time as usual that morning. She acted surprised when Whitey told her that he did not show up at the factory. They were unable to tell if she was hiding anything.

He did not tell her about the IRS agents, figuring that it would be better to wait until he had Casey facing him.

That evening, Whitey and Toni talked about the matter until after one in the morning. They were very concerned over the fact that the IRS could end up taking over the business, and sell it for back taxes. This was exactly what Toni was concerned about when she told Fred not to trust one person with control of the books. She could say I told you so, but that would accomplish nothing.

"What is your next step?" asked Toni.

"All I can do is turn the matter over to our attorney, and hope that he can get us out of this mess. I will go see him this afternoon. In the mean time, I will call and see if Casey is home."

Casey was not home, nor was his wife. His eldest son told Whitey that his father was taken to the hospital with chest pains, and his mother was there with him. The following day, Whitey and his brother drove to St. Jude's Hospital to pay their respects, and to hopefully learn something about the tax monies, but when they arrived they were told that Casey had died early that morning while lying in Intensive Care. Now they would never find out the truth. From that time, it was assumed that Casey knew the Internal Revenue investigators were closing in, and the stress caused his heart attack.

It was never determined if Casey's wife knew anything, so any chance of obtaining leniency from the IRS was highly unlikely, since they considered Whitey to be as guilty as his accountant. At the advice of his attorney, he turned the business over to the IRS for back taxes, and walked away.

Life was never the same for Whitey, and to those who knew him.

Chapter 37

The once happy go lucky big Irishman, was now depressed and turned to drinking heavier than he ever had before. He had taken a job in a small factory as a loom operator, but this was like telling a champion who still had many good years left in him to step down and give up. Many nights after work, Whitey would go to the local pub and drink boiler-makers until he could hardly stand.

When he would arrive home, he would find Toni waiting up because she was worried that he had an accident. She loved him very much, but was at a loss of what to do because no matter how much she tried to help and understand him, his drinking continued uncontrollably, and he was becoming abusive. She had even taken a job working for an interior decorator in the city, so they could make ends meet. She watched her daughter go off to the Navy, and Dolor. follow a year later, because of all the turmoil that had developed at home, from Whitey's excessive drinking. Ronald was the only one of the three children still at home.

He was in the middle of his senior year when his brother joined the Navy, and would only be seventeen when he graduated. He would still be home with his mother to help out and be there for her when times were tough.

More than once, Ronald witnessed his step-father's verbal abuse toward his mother, but said nothing, because it could only make matters worse. There were occasions that Whitey would remain sober for as much as two weeks and life would be pretty good, but unfortunately he would go back to the bottle and the abusiveness.

By the time Ronald had graduated he had seen his dad go from verbal abuse to attempting physical harm on his mom, and that was when he could not just be an observer.

Through his senior year in high school, and until he left to go and live with his sister, who had settled in California with her new husband, Ronald had several verbal and physical encounters with his dad. To Ron, Whitey was his dad, because he was the only father he knew. He was only a year old when his biological father died.

Ron hated the violence and did his best to avoid it, but he was not going to allow anyone to hurt his mother, no matter who they were. On more than one occasion, he stepped in front of his dad, and asked him to leave when it appeared that he might strike his mother. Luckily, for Ron, Whitey did leave without getting physical, because he weighed in at 220 lbs. vs. Ron's 160 lbs.

There were also a couple of occasions, in which Ron did have to defend himself, and only his ability to move quickly saved him. On one occasion, he had just come home from a date and found his mother trying to stop Whitey from striking her with an alarm clock. Ron pushed his way in between the two, and grabbed Whitey's wrists, as he yelled, "God damn you dad what the hell is the matter with you? Mom doesn't deserve this treatment. If you want to hit somebody, try me!"

At that time, Whitey jerked his wrist loose and swung the clock at Ron, who ducked and jumped out of the way; asking his Dad to please stop.

By then, Toni was sobbing and pleading with Fred to settle down and go to bed. Fred looked at her and Ron, dropped the clock, and walked to the living room, with tears in his eyes, where he fell asleep on the sofa.

Chapter 38

For the next three weeks it appeared there was a chance that Whitey's drinking and violence was coming to an end, until one evening when Toni received a call from the Portuguese Club. The owner of the club asked her to have someone come and get Whitey or they would call the police and have him arrested.

Ironically, Dolor had arrived home on leave from the Navy the day before, so when the call came, he volunteered to take Ron and go get Whitey.

Whitey had driven his own car to the club, but evidently became so inebriated that even the club owner, who wanted him removed, wouldn't let him drive, and had fortunately gotten a hold of Whitey's keys. It was also the month of December and the roads were very slick from a storm that had hit earlier. It was dangerous for someone sober to drive, never mind a drunk.

When the boys arrived at the club, they found Whitey standing by the bar ready to take on anyone who was willing to try him. He had already punched the hell out of one individual, who thought he was tough, and he was anxious for another. There was no question about it that it was going to take one hell of a tough guy to control him, and there was no one that stout in the club.

When Dolor and Ron arrived and approached him, Whitey said "I suppose your mother sent you down here to get me."

"That's right Dad, she's worried about you and wants us to bring you home before you get arrested." Dolor responded.

"I don't need any help! I can get home by myself! Go home and tell your mother that I will be home later." Whitey ordered.

"We are not leaving here with out you," said Dolor.

"Please Dad! You have been fighting, and you know that the police will come and arrest you if you don't come with us. You are making mom sick with worry because she loves you and doesn't want to see you in trouble. Common home with us, and let's try to have a good holiday season as a family," pleaded Ron.

"What about my car, who is going to drive it?"

"It will be safe here," said Dolor, looking at the club owner inquisitively.

"That's right! I will be sure that no one bothers it Whitey. Go home with your boys and come back in a day or so, when the roads are safe to drive on."

Saying no more, Fred walked out of the club with the boys at his side until they got to the front of Dolor's vehicle. "I suppose you think that you could have taken me on in there," Whitey said, as he stopped and looked Dolor in the eyes.

"If it came down to that I would have tried," responded Dolor.

"Why don't you try me now," said Fred, shoving Dolor backward.

"Common Dad, let's just get in the car and go home," suggested Ron

"No! I want to see your broth...UH!!! Before Whitey could finish his challenge, Dolor grabbed the lapels of Whitey's coat and with a quick spin threw him onto the hood of the car.

Because the hood was icy, Whitey slid clean over and landed on the ground on the other side where both Ron and Dolor then assisted him to his feet, as Dolor shouted, "God damn it, get into the car Dad. I don't want to fight with you."

Whitey, still catching his breath, got into the back of the car without saying a word and they headed for home. Both boys felt badly about what had taken place. Ron couldn't stop thinking about what he saw his brother do to their father, even though it was done out of necessity, and Dolor was wondering what would have happened if Fred was sober and it became necessary to stand up to him.

At home, Fred went right to bed while Toni and the boys talked about the situation, and hoped for better days ahead. Like many times before, Toni prayed to her statue of the blessed virgin for answers to the turmoil that plagued their lives. Whitey remained sober for the remainder of the holidays, but when he did go on another binge it was like he was trying to make up for lost time.

It was the last Saturday in January, Dolor had returned to his ship, and Jenny was not scheduled to be home on leave until March. Ronald arrived home at midnight, from a date to find his mom sitting in the living room with a look on her face that he had seen quite often. "Dad is out again, isn't he mom?"

"He hasn't come home, since he told us he was going to have the car worked on, at ten o'clock this morning."

"Mom, you have to stop worrying about him so much. It is going to make you sick. You need to get to bed."

"I know it, but it is hard not to worry, when you love someone as much as I love your dad."

"I know mom, but worrying won't help. He will come home when he is damn good and ready. He always makes it home without incident and shows no appreciation for your concern. Common, let's get to bed so we can be rested for tomorrow, and whatever that brings."

Ron said "good night" and went to his room. Shortly after, Toni turned off all but one light and went to her room. At about two in the morning Ron was suddenly awakened from a sound sleep, when he felt a blow to the back of his neck as he lay face down in his bed. The shock caused him to roll onto his side grabbing at the back of his head, as he tried to focus.

"I've got you now you little bastard, and I'm going to teach you some respect!" came a voice in the darkness.

Ron, still groggy and trying to focus on what appeared to be a large figure just about to grab at him, quickly concluded that it was his dad and swung his pillow as hard as he could.

He knocked Whitey off balance, and rolled out of the opposite side of his bed. "Dad you're drunk and don't know what you are doing! Get out of here and go to bed."

"Not before I teach you a lesson! You young punks think you're tough. Well I'm going to show you what tough is."

At that moment, Whitey lunged forward, but Ron shoved the bedroom chair between the both of them, causing Whitey to stumble long enough for him to jump over the bed and get out of the room. "You had better run, because when I catch you, you will know it."

"Cut it out Dad, this is ridiculous. Please go to bed!"

"What is going on?" asked Toni, as she ran from her room, still half asleep.

"Go back to bed this is between your son and me. I am going to teach him a lesson."

"I won't go back to bed! You leave him alone, or I will call the police." No sooner had Toni had her say, Whitey turned to her, attempting to grab her arm.

Seeing this, Ron ran at his dad and shoved him into the wall, yelling, "Get out of here mom! Get out of here!"

Toni ran to the kitchen where the phone was while Ron attempted to control his dad. Walking backward, trying to stay out of Whitey's reach, he worked his way to the front door.

Ron wanted to get Whitey outside, where he could keep his father at bay, until the police arrived. Unfortunately, when he reached the screen door, which he had locked when he came in earlier, it took a second to release the latch and that is when Whitey lunged, driving them both out onto the front landing, partially pulling the screen door from the hinges.

Ron, more stable on his feet, was able to pull from Whitey's grasp. "That's enough, dad. Please stop before the police come and take you to jail," he said, looking down at Whitey who had fallen to one knee.

"Like hell!" responded Fred as he stood, and suddenly lunged for Ron again grabbing him by the arm. I've got you now, you bastard" he yelled, not anticipating that Ron's 160 lbs. was quicker than he anticipated, and soon found out.

No sooner had Whitey gotten a hold of him, Ron used the big man's weight to his advantage, by holding on to his dads forearms and spinning with the same momentum that was used to grab him, causing his dad to go off of the end of the landing on to his left shoulder with all 230 lbs.

"Oh!!! My shoulder, you broke my shoulder!" Whitey exclaimed, as he grasped at the left clavicle with his right hand while rolling on the ground.

About that time, Toni came out, looked at Fred trying to get to his feet and said, "I have called the police so you had better get up and come into the house before they get here and see you making a fool of yourself.

Ron jumped down and assisted Whitey to his feet. It was obvious that his shoulder was injured. It was at least out of place, if not broken.

When the police arrived Whitey was sitting at the kitchen table holding ice to the top of his shoulder. By now he had sobered up a bit, and appeared ashamed for what had taken place. The officers, friends of Whitey, as were most of the police force, advised him that they would have to arrest him if he continued his actions, because they were getting to many complaints about his drunken activities. They suggested that he go to emergency for his shoulder, but he convinced them that he could wait until later that morning, after he had some sleep.

The officers asked Toni if she would be alright "I am not worried, now that he has had the wind knocked out of his sails. I will be Ok!" responded Toni.

Whitey's drinking stopped for about 6 weeks, until one Friday, when some of his cronies invited him to have one drink before going home.

That one drink, led to 2, then 4, and so on and so forth, until he became so inebriated that some of the bar patrons had to carry him to his car. His crony friends left after they suckered him into paying for their drinks.

It was about one a.m. when he reached home, which in itself was a miracle, considering the narrow country roads, together with his impaired vision and slow reflexes. Between the car and the back door, Whitey fell down at least three times. When he finally got into the house, he stumbled into a lamp and knocked it over, causing Toni to wake up and check out the situation.

"I was afraid of this when you didn't come home by dinner time. You are not getting into my bed in that condition." she said.

"Nag, Nag! Why can't you just leave me alone? You always have to say something to aggravate me. I should just shoot you," said Whitey, as he pulled a small revolver from his pocket and pointed it at Toni.

With her heart racing and rapid breathing, Toni was faced with the most frightening situation of her life. She couldn't believe that the man she still loved, dearly, had fallen into such a low ebb. What could she say or do? Ron was still out on a date and here she was all alone, facing a drunk pointing a loaded gun at her.

"Fred, please put the gun down," she pleaded several times.

"Why should I? Can you give me a good reason to go on living?" he responded with tears rolling down his face.

"Yes Fred, I can! We still have the rest of our lives, and the two of us working together, can still make something good out of it if you will only stop drinking so much."

"Dreamer, all you do is dream. It's too late for dreaming. We are getting too old. I think I should end it here and now."

Realizing they were standing by her statue of the Blessed Virgin, Toni fell to her knees with her eyes fixed on the face of Mary, and said, "If that is how you feel Fred, then you are going to have to shoot me in front of the mother of God."

For a good minute, neither one moved and nothing was said, but as if a miracle were happening, Whitey lowered the pistol and placed it on the cabinet top by the statue, as he walked away saying, "Hell, I wouldn't have shot you."

From that time, Whitey tried to curb his drinking, and when he did have a little too much, he would go to bed quietly.

Chapter 39

With all that Toni had to face with Fred, she still had time for her father. Ovid's health had declined rapidly, after Toni moved out, and approximately two years from the time she married Whitey, it was agreed that Raymond, Ovid's youngest son, was in the best situation to take him in. He had been married about a year, and had a large home with no children. The others would each take Ovid to their home one Saturday or Sunday a month, giving Raymond some week ends for him and his wife.

Toni always fulfilled her part of the agreement. When it was her turn, she would always bring her father home for a nice day with her family. She would get him early and take the time to see that he was bathed, his hair trimmed, and his fingernails and toenails were cut. Her brothers and sisters did not render him this kind of treatment, and he was generally in need of her care, by the time she took him.

It was approximately a year after Ovid had moved in with Raymond, that his health had deteriorated so badly, that it became necessary to have him placed in a home for the elderly. From that time, Toni was practically his only visitor.

She would visit him once a week at the facility, and would bring him home for the usual bath and haircut, once a month. Before taking him back, she and Whitey would always take him for a ride and stop for ice cream or apple pie. The other family members, would make it to the home occasionally, but were always making excuses as to why they couldn't give up more time for their father.

It was obvious that Toni still loved her father and was hoping for an indication that he loved her. Unfortunately, he passed on about six months after being placed in the home, and left Toni to never know if he had accepted her as his daughter.

Raymond had been named as the executor and had called the family together for a reading of the will about two weeks after Ovid was buried. Ovid had bequeathed his car and tools to Raymond and the financial portion was to be divided evenly between all of the children, excluding Antoinette (Toni).

Her heart broken, she would no longer have even a slight hope that she was accepted by her father, and now would always wonder if in fact he was. Toni and Fred departed from the reading, with only Roland making an offer to share with her, which she refused. Fred never passed his opinion, but was hurt for Toni and remained cool towards all but Roland for quite some time.

For the next two years, Whitey was pretty good about his drinking. He never stayed on the wagon totally, but the times that he fell off were mild when compared to the past. Like the time that he forced a state trooper into a ditch on Route 44 and ended up in jail. There was the time that he drove over a 30foot embankment, crawled out of the car, and walked 3 miles to wake up Ronald at two in the morning and wanted him to go and pull the car out of the ditch. Whitey still drank too much when there were family outings or it was a holiday, but he stayed at home most of the time which helped to eliminate much of Toni's concern.

It was within those two years, that Jenny and her fiancé David, came home on leave from the Navy, got married and shortly after, transferred to southern California, where Dave was stationed at El Toro Marine Base. Jenny became a housewife after an early discharge from the Navy, due to her pregnancy. At age 19, Ron, wanting to leave the turmoil at home, followed and moved in with Jenny and Dave.

This caused Toni to become lonesome for her children, so she began working on Fred to sell and move to California. "I received a letter from Jenny today, and she says that the temperature has been consistently staying in the mid 80's and they love living there."

They have been going to the beach, and Dave and Ron have been surf fishing. She also said that they are planning to spend Thanksgiving on the beach. Here it is November and we are freezing and will be fighting with old man winter until April or May. Let's sell the house and move to California by next summer." said Toni on a cold November night, while she and Fred were sitting in the living room, watching television.

"California? That is a big move! Shouldn't we at least visit there, before making such a rash decision?" responded Fred.

"That's a good idea! I told Jenny that I would be willing to visit and help her with the new baby which is due in the spring. Let's make reservations to fly out for the birth and we can look around while we are there. We can even see what there is in the way of employment."

"Okay! That sounds good to me, if you think that we can afford it." The idea was appealing to Whitey, since he had spent some time in San Pedro, California when he was working for Munson Shipping Lines as a merchant officer. He thought that he might look up some old mates.

By mid July, that following year, they had sold the house, with one acre, of the 24 it was built on, and left for California.

In April, of that same year, they had spent two weeks with Jenny, her husband Dave, and their new granddaughter and had fallen in love with southern California.

Chapter 40

On August the 1st, 1958, Tony and Whitey arrived in the town of Costa Mesa, California, where they rented a cute apartment in a duplex with great California atmosphere, and which just happened to be next door to Jenny. One year later, they purchased a well maintained, 8 year old home, located just around the corner.

Toni and Whitey couldn't have made a better choice for a home that would fit the bill of grandparents. It was a ranch style home, with a white clap board exterior, and green shutters. The interior was a country atmosphere, of tongue and groove knotty pine walls and ceilings in the living room, with a large stone fireplace, framed by red brick, and a mantle made of oak. T he dinning room was also knotty pine, and had a built in hutch, where Toni kept her crystal.

The floors, throughout, were highly polished hard wood, and were covered with large braided rugs, that Toni had made, when she lived in New England. There were 3 bedrooms, 2 bathrooms, and a nicely lighted kitchen, to which the garage was attached, by a breezeway.

Both Toni and Fred had taken jobs, 6 months after they arrived in California, as neither of them had reached retirement age. Toni went to work in the engineering department of Hughes Aircraft, and Whitey became the lead painter for the Newport School District.

The following 3 years went well for Toni and Fred, and it seemed as if their new life in California was on the way to a smooth retirement until Whitey started coming home from work late, in an inebriated state. Once this started, he soon got back to the 2 or 3 day drunks.

Chapter 41

Ron had returned to Rhode Island, and remained there for 6 months, trying to find his niche in life. He found it lonesome without family and returned to California, to move in with his mom and step-dad until he could find employment. This pleased Toni, not only because she had her son at home again, but also because it helped fill the void that Whitey created when he would go on a drunk.

Dolor was discharged from the Navy in Rhode Island and spent some time there, hoping to marry a childhood sweetheart who eventually dumped him for a guy that he never liked. He moved out to California to live with the family and get over his heart break.

Dolor soon learned what his mother and brother had faced, the 4 years that he spent away from home in the Navy. It was not long before Dolor and Whitey were at each others throat.

Ron eventually became a machinist, and Dolor was employed by U.S. Rubber. Ron took up surfing for a hobby, and Dolor got into searching for gem stones and making jewelry. Jenny of course, was busy being a mother, taking care of 3 children and a new home they had just purchased.

By 1960, Ron met the young lady he thought would be the right one for him, and they married a year later. After their honeymoon, they settled into a one bedroom apartment where a year later, their daughter Karen was born. Life was exciting for the young couple, who were always on the go, surfing, riding dirt bikes, fishing, and having fun with family and friends.

In the mean time, Dolor was still living at home, and his relationship with his step-dad had not improved. It had even gotten to a point one day, that Dolor could no longer control himself, and he socked Whitey in the jaw after Whitey came in drunk and began badgering him about getting out and supporting himself. It was not long after that, Dolor proposed to the young lady he had been dating, and within a year they were married.

Chapter 42

By 1968, Dolor had been employed with a large insurance company, for about 3 years, and had been promoted to their new regional operation in Arizona. The following year, Ron was also transferred to Arizona with the company he had been working for and not to long after, Toni and Fred also moved to Arizona, and retired in Sun City. Jenny and her family remained in California.

At first, the change seemed to help Whitey's drinking problem, since when he did get drunk, he would do it at home and not be out driving. He and Toni enjoyed their life in Arizona, when he was sober, but as time went on, the drinking became increasingly worse, and Whitey's health deteriorated to the point that he became bed ridden and had to be taken care of by Toni. He not only developed cirrhosis of the liver, but gradually developed a brain disorder, and became incapable of communicating and doing for himself. Whitey died at age 74.

Toni eventually sold her condominium, and moved to a luxurious apartment in a high rise for seniors, where she remained for some time before moving in with her son Ron, when living alone became a problem for her. Her daughter Jenny retired and settled in a quiet community in Anaheim Hills, California.

Dolor, the oldest of the two boys, a retired executive from a large insurance company, remained in Tempe, Arizona with his wife, where they live in their modest, paid for home.

Ron, a self employed insurance investigator for the last ten years of 27 in his profession, sold his business and moved to Alaska with his wife Gina, a school teacher. There they set up a residence for almost 10 years. Gina taught and Ron worked with emotionally handicapped boys. On their days off, they played hard in the many adventures that the beautiful state of Alaska has to offer. They fished and hiked in the wilderness in the summer, and worked with Joe Redington, the father of the Iditarod Dog Sled Race, on various Iditarod projects in the winter, besides down hill and cross country skiing, as much as possible.

At age 77, Toni ventured to Alaska, and spent the summer with Ron and Gina. Age was not a factor for her, in looks or physical condition, and she was game to adventure along with whatever her son and daughter-in-law had chosen to do. The highlight of her trip was when she caught a 45lb. king salmon by herself from a drift boat on the famous Kenai River. She also took a flight in a bush float plane to a glacier, where the pilot landed the plane, and she had a glass of champagne over a piece of glacial ice.

Four years later, Toni returned to Alaska with her daughter Jenny. Her age of 81 had not slowed her any, as they traveled to see the sites, and fished. Her attitude on life and her awareness of the importance exercising and eating healthy kept her young at heart, and physically strong. At age 83 she took a Caribbean Cruise and at age 86, she took a trip to Reno, Nevada, for the excitement of the casino night life, and the enjoyment of beautiful Lake Tahoe.

Chapter 43

By age 92 Toni began realizing some physical situations that concerned her. On more than one occasion, she had fallen at the store or in the parking lot. She also fell when walking to her resident dinning room. It seemed that dizziness would suddenly come over her and down she would go. That year, Toni moved in with Ron and Gina. She seemed to improve in strength and continued to drive her old Oldsmobile for another year and then decided to stop driving when her license had to be renewed.

Toni remained relatively strong for her age and enjoyed getting out to a dinner and a little gambling on occasion, but as time passed, she seemed to enjoy the peacefulness of her own setting room over going out.

She had been with Ron and Gina for about three years, when she began complaining about pains in her right side after eating. At first the pain was thought to be indigestion, but when it became persistent, Ron took Toni to see her doctor who was negligent in his diagnosis, when he said "She looks good for her age."

With that, Ron took his mom to his doctor the next day and fortunately, his doctor immediately recognized that Toni was anemic, so he ordered blood tests. Two days later, Ron was told that his mother had cancer and she needed to enter the hospital that week.

Ron related the heart wrenching news to Toni and without

hesitating, she said, "Let's get on with whatever has to be done." Arrangements were made and Toni was admitted the following day. The next day more exams and tests were performed and surgery was scheduled for the following morning. The family was advised of the possibility that Toni might not survive due to her age, but also that the doctors felt relatively confident of success because of her positive attitude. The morning of the surgery, Toni was given expressions of love from her children as she was transported to the surgery facility.

For over two hours, Toni's three children, their spouses and Todd, Ron's son and Todd's spouse Andrea, waited anxiously for the surgeon to come out with an answer on the surgical result, but unexpectedly, a nurse showed and asked the family to follow her to the recovery room where Toni was observed lying in bed surrounded by three nurses and a heart specialist.

She was hooked to a heart monitor and had an oxygen mask on. She was obviously not aware of her situation, but when a relative would grasp her hand she would squeeze back as if to show appreciation. The heart specialist called Ron aside, since he had been designated her executor, and explained that he doubted Toni would make it through the day. Ron responded, "Don't count her out, she is tough."

Toni did make it through the day and after seven more days was sent to a center for rehabilitation and after ten days there, was transported home. Ron was told that it was doubtful she would ever be strong enough to walk again, but within a two weeks of therapy at home, mostly by Ron's wife Gina, Toni began walking with a walker, and eventually she was able to go to dinner and do a little gambling at the local casinos. Most of the time, she maintained a positive attitude.

There were days that Toni was hard to please because she was obviously uncomfortable. Ron and Gina tried hard to accept her periods of unpleasantness, but the last year became unbearable more times than not.

Toni remained with them for a total of five and one half years until her daughter came one day, and abruptly moved her out to her home in California. Needless to say, friction had developed between the three siblings regarding the care of their mother.

In a very short time after the move to California, Toni was placed in a home for the elderly, allegedly due to friction that had developed between her and her daughter. The new home was clean and comfortable, and though Toni often expressed her dissatisfaction about being placed there by her daughter who had often said she would take her in, she eventually adjusted to her situation. When Ron would visit her from Nevada, she often mentioned her disillusionment over her daughter's children, because they had never been to visit her, yet many of her items that were moved to California had been shared with them and not with Ron's children. Even Ron's daughter, her husband, and their two daughter's, had visited her on occasion and brought her ice cream, her favorite desert.

Ron and Gina would take Toni out to breakfast and dinner whenever they would visit and even took her to a movie and out for ice cream, which pleased her to no end, since she had spent most of her time just setting in her room watching TV. On their last visit from Nevada, about nine weeks prior to Toni's 100th birthday, Ron and Gina drove her to the home of their daughter Karen DuBois, in Mission Viejo, California where they spent the day at pool side enjoying the sun and watching Toni's two great granddaughters, Ashlee and Jessica, frolicking in the pool. There, while Toni was watching the girls in the pool and could not hear the conversation, Ron and Karen and their spouses discussed the preparation of a surprise 100th birthday party that would be poolside at Karen's home not expecting the unexpected.

One month away from the planned day for an exciting and fun time, Toni fell and broke her hip. Coincidently, Ron called to speak with his mom only a few minutes after she had fallen and he asked the house person to give her the phone. While still lying on the floor waiting for the ambulance, Toni spoke as if it was not anything to worry about, and even asked of Ron's health as she was aware that he is a diabetic.

During their brief conversation, it once again became apparent that she had no intentions of yielding to a bad situation and said to Ron, "If my hip is broken, it will just have to be repaired." That afternoon, she was informed that surgery would be necessary, and the following morning the procedure was completed successfully.

During the recovery period, Toni had to overcome pneumonia and a few other complications. Ron kept in touch by phone, and when she was four weeks away from her one hundredth birthday, Toni told Ron that she is going to do her best to reach that day for which a special celebration had been planned.

On her 100th birthday, Ron's two siblings threw their mom a nice party, and the following weekend, Ron, his children, and grandchildren threw Toni another 100th birthday celebration. For the following three weeks, Ron kept in touch by phone.

Until the last week of November, Toni seemed spry at times, but said she was ready for God to take her. The last week, prior to her passing on, Toni told Ron that she no longer wanted to exist in her state. Two days after his call she fell into a coma and was pronounced dead the morning of third day. I have no doubt that Toni will remain unyielding in the hereafter.

ROE Author